THE MIDDLE EAST CONFLICT

THE ORIGIN OF JEW HATRED

The Middle East Conflict: The Origin of Jew Hatred

Copyright © 2025 Goose Creek Publishing

All rights reserved. No part of this book may be reproduced or transmitted in any form or by any means, electronic or mechanical, including photocopying, recording, or any information storage and retrieval system, without permission in writing from the publisher.

Unless otherwise noted, all Scripture quotations are taken from the New King James Version®. Copyright © 1982 by Thomas Nelson. Used by permission. All rights reserved.

Scripture quotations marked NIV are taken from the Holy Bible, New International Version®, NIV®. Copyright © 1973, 1978, 1984, 2011 by Biblica, Inc.™ Used by permission of Zondervan. All rights reserved worldwide. www.zondervan.com The "NIV" and "New International Version" are trademarks registered in the United States Patent and Trademark Office by Biblica, Inc.™

Scripture quotations marked NLT are taken from the *Holy Bible*, New Living Translation, copyright © 1996, 2004, 2015 by Tyndale House Foundation. Used by permission of Tyndale House Publishers, Carol Stream, Illinois 60188. All rights reserved.

ISBN: 979-8-9909531-2-3

Assembled and Produced for Goose Creek Publishing by
Breakfast for Seven
breakfastforseven.com

Printed in the United States of America.

THE MIDDLE EAST CONFLICT

THE ORIGIN OF JEW HATRED

JOHN HAGEE

GOOSE CREEK
PUBLISHING

Now Amalek came and fought with Israel in Rephidim. And Moses said to Joshua, "Choose us some men and go out, fight with Amalek. Tomorrow I will stand on the top of the hill with the rod of God in my hand." So Joshua did as Moses said to him, and fought with Amalek. And Moses, Aaron, and Hur went up to the top of the hill. And so it was, when Moses held up his hand, that Israel prevailed; and when he let down his hand, Amalek prevailed.

But Moses' hands *became* heavy; so they took a stone and put *it* under him, and he sat on it. And Aaron and Hur supported his hands, one on one side, and the other on the other side; and his hands were steady until the going down of the sun. So Joshua defeated Amalek and his people with the edge of the sword.

Then the LORD said to Moses, "Write this *for* a memorial in the book and recount *it* in the hearing of Joshua, that I will utterly blot out the remembrance of Amalek from under heaven." And Moses built an altar and called its name, The-LORD-Is-My-Banner; for he said, "Because the LORD has sworn: the LORD *will have* war with Amalek from generation to generation."

EXODUS 17:8-16

CONTENTS

A Message from the Pastor X

Black Sabbath 1
- The Three-Phase Hostage Deal
- The Release
- CUFI Takes Action

Israel's Seven-Front War 19

The Puppet Master and its Puppets 23
- Judea and Samaria
- Assad Ousted
- Peace Through Strength

Anti-Zionism is Antisemitism 33
- March for Israel

Amalek 45

The War Against the Jews 49

Early Antisemitism 53

Haman's Final Solution 59

The Greeks and the Romans 63

The Pharisees, the Sadducees, the Essenes, and Zealots ... 69
- The Great Revolt

The Church Fathers and Judaism 77
- Constantine and the Council of Nicaea
- Triumphalism

- Supersessionism
- John Chrysostom
- Martin Luther
- John Calvin

Crusades, Pogroms, and Ghettos 93
- The Pogroms
- The Ghettos

Myths and Lies 103
- Jew Hatred Begins With Words
- Jews Spread Disease
- Blood Libel
- Deicide
- World Domination
- Holocaust Denial

Post-World War I Germany 115
- Nuremberg Laws

The Night of Broken Glass 123

The Undesirables 127

World War II 133

Hitler's Final Solution 139
- The Wannsee Conference

The Silent Church 143

The Sin of Indifference 149

One Man Had Two Sons 153

The Title Deed 157
- The Abrahamic Covenant
- The Genesis 12 Promise

The Jewish State 165
- The Jewish Question
- Judea

100 Years of Terror 171

The Balfour Declaration 175
- The British Mandate for Palestine
- The Peel Commission
- The British White Paper of 1939

Israel's Right to Exist 181

The Mizrahi Jews 185

The Evolution of Antisemitic Terrorism and Propaganda 189

The Muslim Brotherhood 193

The Palestinian Liberation Organization 197
- Black September
- The Popular Front for the Liberation of Palestine
- Yasser Arafat
- The Lone Wolf
- Pay to Slay

Hezbollah 207

Al Qaeda 213

ISIS 217

Hamas 219
- What Went Wrong

The Houthis 225

Iran 229
- The Iran Deal
- Iran and the Nuclear Bomb

American Leadership and Israel: 2016–Present 235
- It's Biblical

Antisemitism is Everyone's Problem 245

Israel is Eternal 253

What Now? 257

Endnotes 266

Learn More 273

About John Hagee 274

INTRODUCTION
A Message from the Pastor

Jew hatred is a demonic evil that began in the genesis of time and continues until this day. To understand, confront, and eradicate this vile spirit, we must understand the spiritual and historical roots of antisemitism.

This book solemnly explores one of society's oldest and most pervasive forms of sin. I invite you to embark on a journey through the dark corridors of history and into the shadowy corners of the human mind, where hatred toward God's Chosen People resides.

I have dedicated my life to preaching the Gospel of Jesus Christ and fostering the spirit of love, unity, and understanding between the church and Israel. Sadly, I have seen firsthand the devastating impact of hatred, particularly against our Jewish brothers and sisters.

This deep-seated bigotry for the Jewish people is not a relic of the past. It is a living, breathing wickedness that rears its ugly head in various forms, from subtle comments to deadly violence. We must realize that to harbor hatred against the Jews is to reject the very origins of our Christian faith.

Jew hatred or antisemitism is a direct affront to the divine covenant that God made with Abraham, Isaac, and Jacob and their descendants. This unmerited hatred is a blight on humanity that contradicts the teachings of Christ, who was born into a Jewish family and who fulfilled the Old Testament prophecies of the long-awaited Messiah.

> **Jew hatred or antisemitism is a direct affront to the divine covenant that God made with Abraham, Isaac, and Jacob and their descendants.**

> The hatred of God's Chosen People is a sin, and as sin, it damns the soul.

This book traces the historical roots of antisemitism, starting with Amalek's attack on the Israelites and continuing through the deadly rise of Hamas. It examines the current wave of anti-Israel rhetoric and propaganda that is spreading worldwide. In light of the half-truths and blatant lies surrounding the ongoing Seven-Front War that Israel is facing, this book also provides an account of the Swords of Iron Offensive.

I have compiled and condensed a portion of my research on antisemitism from several of my writings on the subject. This manuscript chronicles the ancient roots of Jew hatred and reflects on its present manifestations. It serves as a call to action for every believer who seeks to walk in the light of God's truth. Christians must confront and condemn antisemitism wherever it appears — in our communities, our educational institutions, our churches, and within our circles of influence.

Through prayer and education, coupled with resolute and unconditional support for the Jewish people, we can take action by standing against the injustice of antisemitism and working toward a future where love triumphs over hate and light overcomes this ever-present darkness.

Let us remember the words of Saint Paul in his letter to the Romans:

> *For if the firstfruit is holy, the lump is also holy; and if the root is holy, so are the branches.*
> *(Romans 11:16)*

His message? Judaism doesn't need Christianity to explain its existence; however, Christianity must have Judaism to explain ours.

Our sacred duty is to honor, comfort, and bless God's Chosen People.

...For if the Gentiles have been partakers of their spiritual things, their duty is also to minister to them in material things.
(Romans 15:27)

May the Lord bless and keep you, and may His wisdom direct you in the fight against the evil of Jewish hatred. Together, we can dispel the darkness by shining the unconditional light of the love of God.

Then I saw that wisdom excels folly as light excels darkness.
(Ecclesiastes 2:13)

Pastor John Hagee

CHAPTER 1

Black Sabbath

The Black Sabbath Massacre of October 7, 2023, was Israel's darkest moment since the nation was reborn over 77 years ago, and for the Jewish people, it was the deadliest day since the Holocaust.

October 6, 2023, ended like any other day in Israel — then abruptly, the entire world was changed forever. As the Sabbath's early morning sun gently kissed the rolling farmland and small towns of southern Israel, peace and tranquility were shattered by the wail of incoming rocket fire.

Families in Israel's southern kibbutz villages were violently awakened, and like countless times before, they

> October 6, 2023, ended like any other day in Israel — then abruptly, the entire world was changed forever.

believed they had seconds to grab their little ones and race into bomb shelters. They believed that once inside, they would be safe. They believed that Israel's high-tech missile defense shield would intercept the rockets.

That same morning, in the Negev desert, the sound of sirens interrupted the Nova Music and Peace Festival held in Re'im. Festival goers scrambled to find shelter and anticipated, just like those in the kibbutzim, that the rockets would be intercepted, and before long, all would continue as planned.

They all believed they would live to see the sunset that day and that their lives would continue with peace and prosperity. They were wrong.

While Jews around the globe were preparing to commemorate Simchat Torah, marking the completion of the annual reading of the first five books of Moses, a horrible evil was taking place in God's Promised Land.

Beginning at 4:30 AM on October 7, 2023, Palestinian terrorists launched a massive barrage of rockets into Israel, triggering sirens as far as Tel Aviv and Jerusalem.

Reports concluded that Hamas, the radical Iranian-backed Palestinian terrorist group based in Gaza, violated an existing ceasefire by initiating a horrific attack on the Jewish nation. Intending to overwhelm the Israeli missile defense systems, Hamas and its allies fired up to 5,000 rockets at southern Israel. However, this vast missile barrage was only a diversion of the evil to come.

At around 6:30 AM, a significant escalation occurred when Hamas launched a multi-faceted attack on Israel, affecting land, air, and sea. The militants used bulldozers to breach parts of the defense wall separating Gaza from southern Israel, enabling many of them to enter on motorcycles and trucks. At the same time, others flew over the border using paragliders, while Palestinian forces breached Israel's maritime border by motorboat near the scenic coastal town of Zikim.

Radical terrorists continued to launch attacks on Israel Defense Forces (IDF) bases near the Gaza border, resulting in the deaths or capture of Israeli soldiers. They utilized various tactics to disrupt communications, which slowed the IDF's response to these attacks. Hamas specifically targeted cellphone towers, destroying them as they infiltrated into Israel. In addition, they conducted waves of cyberattacks and jammed radio frequencies, leading to a near-total communications blackout in southern Israel.

Six thousand Gazans breached the border in 119

> **Radical terrorists continued to launch attacks on Israel Defense Forces (IDF) bases near the Gaza border, resulting in the deaths or capture of Israeli soldiers.**

different locations that morning. Among the assailants were 3,800 "elite Nukhba forces" and an added 2,200 radical Palestinians. Additionally, 1,000 Hamas militants fired thousands of rockets from the Gaza Strip into Israel, bringing the total number of Hamas' demonic warriors to 7,000.[i]

No one could have predicted the horror that was to unfold in the subsequent hours as Hamas terrorists infiltrated peaceful farms and communities. The crazed attackers engaged in barbarity similar to the pogroms of decades past. They went from house to house, murdering families in cold blood, taking hostages, and engaging in horrific abuses. At the same time, 260 Nova participants were massacred as Hamas savages proudly celebrated the heinous crimes they were committing by recording and parading their atrocities on their social media outlets.

> On their orchestrated path of destruction, Hamas slaughtered over 1,200 people and wounded over 5,400 more.

These innocent victims never saw evening's sunset; instead, men, women, and children were sexually violated, tortured, dismembered, burned alive, shot, and brutally murdered. Whole families were wiped out while others were taken to Gaza. This demonic spawn showed no mercy — not even the infants were spared.

The dead, the captives, or the wounded...should not be remembered as mere numbers — they are mothers, fathers, daughters, sons, brothers, sisters, babies, and even the unborn. One moment, the victims were gathered at a music festival, peacefully sleeping in their beds, at their breakfast tables, or preparing to celebrate the final reading cycle of the Torah and the beginning of the new day by dancing in their synagogues — and the next moment — they lay dead, dying, or missing.

In the subsequent chaotic hours of the Hamas invasion, Israeli security forces managed to eliminate the terrorists that remained inside the southern Jewish communities. On October 8, Israeli Prime Minister Benjamin Netanyahu declared war on Hamas with these words, *"Citizens of Israel, we are at war. This is not an operation or ground fighting. This is a war and we will win!"*

With the approval of its Security Cabinet, Jerusalem launched *Operation Swords of Iron*, intended to bring the hostages home and destroy Hamas. Within hours, an unprecedented number of 360,000 Israeli military reservists reported for active duty, the most rapid mobilization in Israel's history.

In addition to the 1,200 dead, 251 Israeli and foreign civilians and IDF soldiers, some alive and

> **"Citizens of Israel, we are at war. This is not an operation or ground fighting. This is a war and we will win!"**

others dead, were taken into Gaza on October 7. The hostages, ranging in age from 1 to 86, were scattered throughout the Gaza Strip in homes or in the Hamas-built underground hellscapes, which were cramped, damp, and unbearable.[ii]

Hamas' stated goal was and is to force Israel to exchange Israeli hostages for radical Palestinian prisoners. We must not forget the innocent Israeli captives that remain or their families that are praying every day for their safe return.

THE FOLLOWING IS THE TIMELINE OF THEIR PLIGHT:

OCTOBER 7, 2023	Hamas takes 251 hostages into Gaza.
OCTOBER 20, 2023	Hamas releases two Israeli-American hostages.
OCTOBER 23, 2023	Hamas releases two elderly Israeli hostages.
OCTOBER 30, 2023	Israeli forces rescue an Israeli soldier.
NOVEMBER 21, 2023	Israel and Hamas agree to a seven-day

truce through intermediaries from Egypt and Qatar. Approximately half of the Israeli hostages were released in exchange for three times that number of terrorists held in Israeli prisons. Despite international pressure to extend the ceasefire, Hamas once again violated the agreement, leading to a resumption of fighting.

FEBRUARY 12, 2024 — The IDF rescues two hostages from Hamas' captivity.

JUNE 8, 2024 — The IDF launched Operation Arnon, a dramatic hostage rescue of four hostages from the Nuseirat refugee camp, including Noa Argamani, whose haunting abduction video circulated through international media.

AUGUST 27, 2024 — The IDF rescued Qaid Farhan al-Qadi, an Israeli-Bedouin, from the dark tunnels in Gaza.

LATE AUGUST, 2024 — Six hostages were brutally murdered by Hamas terrorists as IDF soldiers neared their location. Included was American Hersh Goldberg-Polin, whose mother, Rachel, became a symbol of strength and

	resilience in advocating for the release of her only son and all the hostages.
PLEASE NOTE	No hostages were released by Hamas in 2024.
JANUARY 1, 2025	At least 94 hostages are still being held in Gaza; one-third of them are believed to be dead.
JANUARY 15, 2025	A hostage deal is agreed upon by Israel and Hamas.

THE THREE-PHASE HOSTAGE DEAL

Through months of painstaking negotiations, Hamas constantly attempted to extort more concessions by walking away from the table. However, Qatari and American mediators announced that a Gaza ceasefire and an Israeli hostage release deal had been agreed upon.

Hamas leaders claimed victory and praised the October 7 Massacre as a significant achievement that would be taught to future generations of Palestinians with pride.

Hamas once again showed its true face, with no remorse for the attack or the suffering that Gazans have endured because of their actions.

Phase One of the three-phase agreement covers a span of six weeks. It includes the release of 33 hostages, including 12 women and children, men aged 50 and above, and injured civilians, including two Americans.

Phase Two will take place if Israel and Hamas reach an agreement on the terms of the truce. The deal states that negotiations for this second phase will commence 16 days after satisfying Phase One. The objectives of Phase Two include the release of all remaining hostages, the establishment of a permanent ceasefire, and the complete withdrawal of Israeli troops from Gaza.

Phase Three would involve returning the bodies of the remaining dead held hostage in exchange for a Gaza reconstruction plan lasting three to five years, as overseen by international entities.

THE RELEASE

- **January 19, 2025:** After 477 days in captivity, Hamas-led Palestinian militants released three Israeli women: Emily Damari, 28; Romi Gonen, 24; and Doron Steinbrecher, 31. Romi was abducted from the Nova music festival, while Emily and Doron were taken from their homes in Kibbutz Kfar Aza. Their release was part of an exchange for 90 Palestinian prisoners.

- **January 22, 2025:** The Iranian Supreme Leader Ayatollah Khamenei issued his response to the Hostage Deal — "Gaza has Won."

- **January 25, 2025:** Hamas released four Israeli hostages: Naama Levy, Liri Albag, Daniella Gilboa, and Karina Ariev.

- **January 30, 2025:** Three Israeli hostages — Arbel Yehoud, 29, Agam Berger, 19, and Gadi Mozes, 80 — were released. Additionally, five Thai hostages were freed, leaving three Thai nationals, one Nepalese, and one Tanzanian hostage still held in Gaza.

- **February 1, 2025:** Hamas released three more Israeli hostages: Ofer Calderon, Keith Siegel, and Yarden Bibas. While Yarden Bibas was returned home, the status of his wife Shiri and their two children, Kfir, aged 1, and Ariel, aged 5, was not yet known. Additionally, dual Israeli American citizen Sagui Dekel-Chen, 36, was still awaiting his release.

- **February 8, 2025:** Hamas released three additional hostages: Eli Sharabi, Ohad Ben Ami, and Or Levy. The condition of these men was appalling, as they appeared to resemble

Holocaust survivors. As of the 8th, approximately 75 hostages remain in Gaza, with roughly half of them believed to be deceased.

- **February 15, 2025:** Hamas released Russian-Israeli Alexander Troufanov, Argentinian-Israeli Yair Horn, and US-Israeli Sagui Dekel-Chen after concerns over a lasting ceasefire. Approximately 15 months after the October 7, 2023, attacks, Israel says 70 of the 251 hostages remain unaccounted for, and only 35 of these are believed to be alive.

- **February 20, 2025:** Hamas released the bodies of four hostages who were murdered after being taken from Kibbutz Nir Oz. The terrorists paraded their bodies through Gaza in a shocking display of cruelty and propaganda. The victims included Shiri Bibas, 32, and her two sons: Ariel, who was 4, and Kfir, who was just 9 months old at the time of their kidnapping, and 83-year-old Oded Lifshitz. Israeli forensic scientists positively identified the bodies of Ariel, Kfir, and Oded. However, testing revealed that the fourth body received was not that of Shiri Bibas, and no matches were found for any other hostage. This body remains anonymous and unidentified. Israel demanded that Hamas return Shiri home.

- **February 21, 2025:** The body of Shiri Bibas, whose own mother and father were murdered on October 7, 2023, is returned to her homeland.

- **February 22, 2025:** Hamas released Tal Shoham, Omer Shem Tov, Omer Wenkert, and Eliya Cohen; all were kidnapped during the October 7, 2023, attacks. Ethiopian-Israeli Avera Mengistu and Israeli Palestinian Bedouin Hisham al-Sayed were also freed after being held in Gaza for over a decade. The six hostages were released in the final exchange of the first phase of the Israel-Hamas ceasefire.

- **February 26, 2025:** Shiri Bibas and her two sons, who were brutally murdered while in captivity, were laid to rest. Thousands of Israelis lined the streets in tribute to the slain mother and her beloved children. It was noted by a mourner at the funeral, "The terrible massacre crossed generations. It erased in one stroke three generations of the family."

Another mourner, declared, "Today, we are all part of the Bibas family." This is just one heartbreaking story of the over 250 families that were either killed or kidnapped and tortured on that horrible day. How much is too much? When will the evil of Jew hatred be cruel enough before the world says no more?

The same day, Hamas returned the bodies of Itzhak Elgarat, 69; Tsachi Idan, 50; Ohad Yahalomi, 50; and 86-year-old Shlomo Mantzur.

This is the eighth exchange under the first phase of the ceasefire. Nearly half of the 59 hostages that remain in Gaza are believed dead.

- **May 12, 2025:** After 584 days in captivity, Hamas released Edan Alexander, the last living U.S. citizen held in Gaza. Of the 58 hostages who remain, only half are believed to be alive.

The images of the hostages reuniting with their loved ones are vividly imprinted in our minds, representing a glimmer of hope after the dreadful months of darkness. However, the joy of these long-awaited reunions is overshadowed by the ongoing anguish of those still waiting for news about the fate of the remaining hostages, as well as the grief experienced by those who have received the bodies of their cherished family.

Throughout history, the Jewish people have been known for valuing their God-given gift of life. In contrast, Israel's enemies, who celebrate death, perceive this virtue as a weakness in any negotiation process. As a result, Israel's leadership is often forced to make painful and unpopular concessions to protect the lives of its citizens.

Golda Meir, Israel's Prime Minister from 1969 to 1974 and the first female head of state in the Middle East, described the situation this way:

> "Everyone has a right to self-determination, yet we are the only people in the world who have no right to self-determination — we have the right to independence.
>
> The quarrels with the Arabs are not quarrels for a piece of land; they are not for territory or anything concrete. They [Israel's enemies] refuse to believe that we have the right to exist at all. [They say] go back to the borders of '67, and then there will be peace. We were in the borders of '67 — why was there war? Immediately after the war, we said, "Let us sit down and negotiate peace." The Arabs didn't do it.
>
> One of our kibbutzim right across Jordan has been shelled day and night. A father and his little boy went into the shelter, and the child was scared and crying. The father said, "Look, don't worry, these are not the shells from the other side; these are our shells." The child said, "Do they have shelters for the children on the other side?"...It's difficult, and that's why we value life — not only our own, but all life.
>
> This is our strength. Maybe you want to say this is our weakness because Arab leaders are not so sensitive

to the very question of life…to having people alive instead of dead."

The plans for post-war Gaza have not yet been finalized, particularly regarding who will eventually govern the territory. Israel has clearly stated that Hamas, which is committed to its destruction and is dedicated to terrorism, should not be involved in the future governance of Gaza.

Additionally, the Israeli government opposes the participation of the Palestinian Authority, which currently administers parts of the West Bank (Judea and Samaria) while also maintaining its "pay-to-slay" policy that is an inducement to commit murder.

CUFI & HAGEE MINISTRIES TAKE ACTION

On the same morning that Prime Minister Benjamin Netanyahu declared war on Hamas, Christians United for Israel (CUFI) and Hagee Ministries took immediate action by reaching out to various humanitarian organizations in Israel to provide critical emergency aid. To date, we have donated 100% of the over $16.5 million raised to assist the victims of this tragic conflict. This relief effort has included support for the more than a quarter of a million Israelis who were displaced as they fled their homes to escape deadly missile strikes and terrorist attacks.

Since October 7, 2023, Christians United for Israel has hosted 11 trips to Israel, with another 11 scheduled through the end of December 2025, to demonstrate solidarity with the Jewish nation and its people during this difficult time. Our goal is to educate as many students, pastors, professors, school administrators, and influencers as possible with the facts concerning Israel and the Middle East.

In April 2025, Diana, the executive board members, and I participated in the March of the Living. Immediately afterward, we traveled to Israel to witness firsthand the devastation caused by both historic and present-day Jew hatred. We heard heart-wrenching eyewitness accounts from survivors of Hitler's Final Solution as well as Hamas' modern-day carnage.

We walked through the rubble of Israel's ravaged communities, where entire families were tortured, mutilated, and executed. We spoke to hostages who had been set free from the dark hellholes of Gaza and wrapped our arms around family members who are grieving the loss of their loved ones at the hands of Hamas. Our experiences forever changed our group, and we are more committed than ever to combat antisemitism wherever it raises its ugly head and to ensure that this carnage never happens again!

CHAPTER 2

Israel's Seven-Front War

Since October 7, Hamas, Hezbollah, the Houthis of Yemen, Iran, and other Iran-backed terrorist organizations have launched over 25,000 rockets at Israel. Thankfully, Israel's cutting-edge missile defense network (which includes the short-range Iron Dome, medium-range David's Sling, and the long-range Arrow 3) has intercepted the majority of these missiles; however, an untold number of Israelis have been killed or injured.

To date, the IDF has published the names of over 890 soldiers, officers, and reservists who lost their lives in this multi-front war. Among the dead are at least six colonels and six Lt. Colonels marking the highest number of senior officers killed in combat in recent memory.[iii]

On October 27, 2023, Israel launched a full-scale ground offensive into Gaza, intensifying its ongoing conflict with Hamas since the violence began. As Israeli troops engage with Palestinian militants in the densely populated territory, Hamas continues to disgracefully use hospitals, schools, and residential homes as shields for its terrorist operatives and hiding places for its weapons.

> This mission is fraught with danger, as the IDF must balance its operational objectives with the need to protect innocent Gazans and minimize casualties among their own troops.

Israel is determined to make Hamas face severe consequences for its repulsive actions, and as a result, many of its terrorist fighters and leaders have been eliminated. Since the war began, Ismail Haniyeh, the head of Hamas' Political Bureau, was assassinated in Tehran, Iran. Additionally, Yahya Sinwar, the mastermind behind the attacks, was killed in a firefight with Israeli forces on October 16, 2024.

In essence, the Jewish people are fighting their second War of Independence on seven fronts following the Black Sabbath massacre. This war for survival involves Hamas and other militant groups in Gaza; Hezbollah in Lebanon; the Houthis in Yemen; various Iran-backed militias in Iraq and Syria; Palestinian militants in the West Bank; and Iran itself, which directly attacked Israel for the first time in April 2024.

Amid the current circumstances, some truths remain — this battle will not end until every hostage is returned, Hamas is eliminated, and the balance among the players in this war is neutralized.

CHAPTER 3

The Puppet Master and Its Puppets

As stated, the prevailing war has extended beyond Gaza, highlighting the complexities Israel faces in the region. For decades, Iran has supported Hamas and the Palestinian Islamic Jihad, the groups that executed the appalling events of October 7, 2023; however, its deadly tentacles reach even further.

On July 27, 2024, a Hezbollah rocket tragically struck a soccer field in the Israeli Druze town of Majdal Shams, resulting in the deaths of 12 children aged 10 to 16 and injuring over 40 others. This heartbreaking event crossed a critical line, prompting Israel to take a strong stand against the Lebanese branch of this terrorist organization to protect its northern communities.

Days later, Israeli troops entered Lebanon, pushing Hezbollah back from the border and dismantling its terror infrastructure. Lebanese troops retreated from the perimeter, confirming that this was a conflict between Hezbollah and Israel.

In September of 2024, Israel executed a strategic operation to substantially weaken the Hezbollah terror network by detonating thousands of communication devices, including pagers and walkie-talkies, used by its members in Lebanon and Syria. This operation led to the death of at least 40 Hezbollah militants with over 5,000 others wounded.

> **In September of 2024, Israel executed a strategic operation to substantially weaken the Hezbollah terror network.**

Just over a week later, as Hezbollah struggled to regain its footing, its notorious leader, Hassan Nasrallah, was killed in a precise Israeli airstrike. This decisive action marked a pivotal moment in the fight.

By the end of November 2024, a ceasefire brokered by the United States was agreed upon between Israel and Hezbollah. This agreement required Hezbollah to relocate north of the Litani River, while Israeli forces would withdraw from southern Lebanon. Despite the ceasefire, tensions remain high, as Israel has reported multiple violations by the Iranian proxy.

The Houthis of Yemen, also known as Ansar Allah, were designated as a Foreign Terrorist Organization by President Trump just five days after he took office on January 20, 2025. The Houthis are a proxy of Iran's Islamic Revolutionary Guard Corps Quds Force (IRGC-QF), which arms and trains terrorist organizations globally. Since 2023, the Houthis have fired on U.S. Navy warships, posing a threat to American servicemen and women and international shipping in the Red Sea.

Since October 7, 2023, in solidarity with Hamas, Hezbollah, considered the crown jewel of Iran's terrorist network, and the Houthis have launched thousands of missile and drone attacks against Israel. These assaults have resulted in casualties and injuries among Israeli citizens, displacing tens of thousands who have been forced to flee their homes in northern Israel.

Understanding the multifaceted confrontations Israel encounters today is crucial. This resilient nation faces threats from Hamas in the south and Hezbollah in the north, along with various groups in Syria, Yemen, and Iraq. Additionally, ongoing threats from Palestinian terrorists in Judea and Samaria (West Bank) add to this fight.

JUDEA AND SAMARIA

The situation is worsened by the significant influence of the "Iranian Axis," contributing to a cycle of death and destruction. Since the early part of 2025, the Israel Security Agency and the IDF have stopped 90 major terrorist attacks in Judea and Samaria.[iv]

Nonetheless, Israel's strength and resilience stand out amidst these challenges through Operation Iron Wall, which is countering the Iranian-backed militants in the area.

My good friend, former Ambassador to Israel, David Friedman, explains the fragile dynamics of Judea and Samaria:

> "In the immediate aftermath of October 7, 2023, Palestinians in Judea and Samaria were polled to see how they perceived the Hamas massacre. More than 80% of those responding were in favor.
>
> The Palestinian Authority, which purports to govern Palestinian areas within Judea and Samaria, has failed to condemn Hamas. It also maintains a pension system that rewards and incentivizes Palestinian terrorists to kill Jews.
>
> There have been no elections within the Palestinian Territories in Judea and Samaria for nearly 20 years. Current polling indicates that an election would result in a resounding victory for Hamas.

Regardless of whether Hamas or the Palestinian Authority governs within Judea and Samaria, neither has shown the interest nor the capability to rein in terror attacks on Jews, which continue with tragic results to this day."

There is no doubt about it: Israel is actively engaged in a multifaceted struggle for survival.

At the center is the "Puppet Master" of them all — the Iranian regime, which is committed to killing every Jew on the face of the earth. This same regime refers to Israel as the "Little Satan" and America as the "Great Satan."

The animosity and aggression of the Islamic Republic toward the Jewish state have long been evident. However, in April 2024, this hostility escalated to a new level. For the first time in history, Iran's regime launched a direct assault into Israel from its territory. Approximately 170 drones, more than 30 cruise missiles, and over 120 ballistic missiles were fired at Israel during this orchestrated attack.

Thanks to God's intervention, Israel's aerial defense systems, and a coalition that included the United States, Great Britain, Saudi Arabia, and Jordan, 99% of the Iranian projectiles were intercepted. In response, Israel conducted limited, targeted strikes on high-value Iranian targets. While aerial footage from Iran showed the crushing aftermath of these strikes, the Iranian regime denies that any such actions took place to maintain its image among its citizens.

As Iran's Islamic regime faced even more challenges following the removal of its top terror leaders, Haniyeh and Nasrallah, it launched a second and even larger ballistic missile attack on Israel on October 1, firing over 180 projectiles. Fortunately, Israel's air defense systems successfully intercepted the majority of the missiles, resulting in only one fatality — a Palestinian man who was killed by falling debris from a rocket.

Sixteen days later, Israel retaliated by striking approximately 20 Iranian-affiliated targets across Iran, Iraq, and Syria. This decisive action significantly weakened Iran's future capability to target Israel and to defend itself against potential Western retaliation. After significant damage to the leadership and military forces of Hamas and Hezbollah, and following Israel's successful strike on Iran — during which Israeli jets operated freely in Iranian airspace — the Islamic Republic would face yet another blow before the end of 2024.

ASSAD OUSTED

In December 2024, after 13 years of a brutal civil war and a multi-billion-dollar infusion of support from Iran and Russia, the Syrian totalitarian regime came to an end with the fall of Bashar al-Assad.

This offensive, led by Hay'at Tahrir al-Sham (HTS), a U.S.-designated Foreign Terrorist Organization (FTO) since 2018, captured Aleppo within just a week, as city after city fell to the advancing rebels as Assad's army retreated. The battle ended in 11 days, culminating in the rebels taking Damascus. The era of Bashar al-Assad's oppressive rule ended as he fled to Moscow.

Iranian agents have also fled Syria, signaling the end of the long-standing strategic alliance between Tehran and Damascus. The future of Syria is now uncertain. Will a government that genuinely serves the Syrian people emerge, or will Israel continue to confront another radical Islamist threat at its border?

What happens next in the region remains uncertain. However, the fall of Assad has compelled the Iranian regime to pull back primarily within its borders. Israel's counterattack following the October 7 massacre significantly weakened Iran's aggressive ambitions for supremacy in the Middle East despite the influx of revenue as a result of the Biden administration's lack of sanctions enforcement.

> **Israel's counterattack following the October 7 massacre has significantly weakened Iran's aggressive ambitions for supremacy in the Middle East.**

PEACE THROUGH STRENGTH

In February 2025, Prime Minister Benjamin Netanyahu visited the White House as the first foreign leader to do so in the new administration. During the official visit, President Trump laid out a vision that challenges our Arab partners to drastically change the status quo in Gaza, which has resulted in death and destruction for Israelis and Palestinians.

The historic meeting also culminated with several executive actions by the president to strongly ramp up economic and diplomatic pressure against Iran, fight Jew hatred at home, pull the U.S. out of antisemitic international organizations, and provide Israel with the means to defend itself against our shared enemies.

President Trump also warned the Iranians that he had given his advisers instructions for Iran to be "obliterated" if it assassinates him – something Iran has been seeking to do for years. At the same time, President Trump has made it clear to Tehran's leaders that they can choose a diplomatic path to end the war while he pursues his "peace through strength" vision.

The Ayatollah is under pressure as the Trump administration has given our government and the Israeli government the means with which to pursue the required paths to ensure that Iran can never reach its nuclear weapon goals.

We know that genuine peace hinges on strength, and the Iranians have repeatedly shown that they only respond when unflinching power is exhibited. Ensuring that Iran can never threaten the United States or Israel with nuclear weapons requires nothing short of that.

Our daily prayer is that by the time you read this book, the conflict has ended, Hamas has been dismantled, and all the hostages have returned safely to their families. But if not, we still celebrate the joy of those families who have welcomed their loved ones back and mourn for those whose relatives remain captive or who were murdered by Hamas' brutality.

The regime in Tehran bears as much responsibility for the atrocities committed on October 7 as the barbarians who carried out the heinous acts. Despite this fact, countless misinformed people have opted to direct their anger toward Israel. In the immediate aftermath of the brutal Black Sabbath Massacre, crowds of pro-Hamas supporters celebrated around the globe, leading to a spike in antisemitic threats and attacks, including here in the United States.

We know, however, all too well that as long as the Puppet Master and its puppets hold air in their lungs and weapons in their hands, they will always seek to threaten the United States and Israel. The war that began on October 7 may soon be coming to a close, but the war between good and evil in the Middle East unfortunately remains.

CHAPTER 4

Anti-Zionism is Antisemitism

Hatred against God's Chosen People did not begin with this war. History has proven that antisemitism has been an ever-present shadow in our global society. However, these evil attacks against the Jewish nation and her people exposed its evil and ever-growing existence.

In the days and weeks that followed October 7, hateful demonstrations expressing vile antisemitism and violence erupted worldwide. At the same time, there was a deafening silence in defense of the women who were viciously violated during the invasion, and condemnation for the random and brutal butchering of children and infants was nonexistent.

Instead, while Israel was mourning their dead and still searching for the missing, hundreds of thousands of radicals around the globe took to the streets in support of Hamas and their gruesomely murderous acts.

Less than a week after the massacre, Hamas called on *"all of its supporters to hold a 'Day of Rage,'"* urging their followers to *"attack Israelis and Jews"* the world over. Once again, the Jewish people found that any sense of security or peace vanished overnight, and once again, they were fighting for survival in the battle of good against evil.

In Yemen, demonstrators crowded the streets waving Yemeni and Palestinian flags, shouting their slogan, *"Allah is the greatest; death to America; death to Israel; the curse of the Jews; victory to Islam."* Egyptian protestors surrounded the Al-Azhar Mosque in Cairo, chanting that Israel remained their enemy from *"generation after generation."*

One of Iraq's political leaders, Shiite cleric Muqtada al-Sadr led tens of thousands of protesters in Baghdad's Tahrir Square. Anti-Israel demonstrators flooded the streets across Iran and in Tehran, burning Israeli and

American flags, chanting, *"Death to Israel," "Death to America," "Israel will be doomed,"* and *"Palestine will be the conqueror."*

In Beirut, thousands of supporters of Lebanon's Hezbollah terror group waved Lebanese, Palestinian, and Hezbollah flags, chanting slogans in support of Gaza and calling for *"death to Israel."* From the usually quiet streets of Amman, Jordan, to the Syrian capital of Damascus and Pakistan's capital of Islamabad, Friday prayer worshipers poured into the streets and trampled on American and Israeli flags.[v]

Europe was no different. Following the tragic events of October 7, Europe has seen a disturbing rise in antisemitic incidents, including threats to Jewish shops and attacks on synagogues, as well as demonstrations calling for Israel's eradication. It was a resurrection of the European pogroms of the past.

In Russia, there was an attempted pogrom when a mob of assailants stormed the airport in Dagestan, searching for Jews to lynch after learning that a flight from Israel was arriving. The media reported that the attackers stopped cars outside the airport, demanding to see documents in their search for Israeli passports.

On November 6–7, 2024, Jewish people and pro-Israel advocates expressed deep horror and outrage over a violent, widespread, and seemingly premeditated antisemitic attack on Israeli soccer fans in Amsterdam during a match between Maccabi Tel Aviv and Ajax, the most successful soccer team in the Netherlands.

Israeli attendees were hunted down and brutally assaulted. The assailants, taking their cue from Hamas terrorists, videoed their attacks, showing Jews fearfully scrambling for safety amid the violent mob. Some hid for hours, and others jumped into canals to save themselves.

While this incident happened after a soccer match in Europe, it highlights a concerning global trend of skyrocketing antisemitism impacting Jews, Israelis, and Zionists everywhere. The alarming support for terrorism by groups like Hamas, Hezbollah, the Palestinian Authority, and the Houthis is frightening and often tolerated and condoned across many regions of the world, including the U.S.

Our nation is no exception. Since the Hamas attack, Jewish Americans have been subject to levels of antisemitism not seen in decades. The Anti-Defamation League reported that well over 3,000 antisemitic incidents took place across the United States between October 7, 2023, and January 7, 2024 — triple the number of recorded incidents during the entire calendar year of 2022.

Shamefully, many of America's city streets, state capitals, college campuses, and even the Halls of Congress — where Jewish people freely walked just days before — became places of fear and intimidation following October's massacre.

> **Antisemitic rallies, threats, and attacks against the Apple of God's Eye occurred throughout our nation, including radical pro-Hamas demonstrations on college campuses.**

During a three-month period, America's institutions of higher learning experienced over 500 antisemitic incidents. This marked a 700% increase in the number of anti-Jewish incidents on campus from October to February compared to the same period a year earlier.

Anti-Israel "encampments" that began at Columbia University spread unchallenged across the nation. These camps became centers of anti-Jewish and anti-American sentiment, contributing to a worsening antisemitic climate on campuses.

Many college administrations allowed these hostile encampments to spew their venom while tuition-paying Jewish students were banned from certain areas of the same campuses. Notable exceptions included the

University of Florida and Texas A&M, which enforced a zero-tolerance policy for pro-Hamas agitators.

Several universities have updated their policies regarding disruptive demonstrations in response to the damaging effects of recent anti-Israel protests, which resulted in significant financial losses of alumni support. Institutions such as Cornell University, the University of California system, the University of Michigan, and the University of Pennsylvania have implemented new regulations, including prohibiting tents, banning megaphones, and requiring permits for gatherings in communal spaces.

The University of Michigan has also expanded its administration's authority to impose disciplinary actions on students participating in these protests.[vi]

On the subject of antisemitism, HHS Secretary Robert F. Kennedy Jr. said, "Antisemitism — like racism — is a spiritual and moral malady that sickens societies and kills people with lethalities comparable to history's most deadly plagues. In recent years, the censorship and false narratives of woke cancel culture have transformed our great universities into greenhouses for this deadly and virulent pestilence."

Additionally, Education Secretary Linda McMahon said, "Americans have watched in horror for more than a year now, as Jewish students have been assaulted and harassed on elite university campuses. Unlawful encampments and demonstrations have completely paralyzed day-to-day campus operations, depriving Jewish students of learning opportunities to which they are entitled."[vii] Clearly, antisemitism education is desperately needed at the university level.

Antisemitism in some of America's educational institutions did not arise suddenly; instead, it has been openly and unapologetically fostered on many college campuses that receive funding from anti-Israel countries. A recent study revealed that from 1981 to 2020, Arab nations donated approximately $10 billion to American schools, with about 40% of this total going unreported.

> **Clearly, antisemitism education is desperately needed at the university level.**

Qatar, Saudi Arabia, the United Arab Emirates, and Kuwait are the most prominent university donors; notable institutions like Harvard, Columbia, Yale, Cornell, and Georgetown were among the recipients. These contributions established research centers, endowed chairs, and academic programs on Islamic, Arab, and Palestinian issues.

Do these grants promote a better understanding between Jews and Arabs?

Are they accurately teaching the true geopolitical history of the Middle East?

Do they offer insights into the Jewish and Muslim faiths or the possibility of peace in our time?

No! Instead, they indoctrinate the next generation in Jew hatred.

Much of the Jewish hatred within academia stems from its leadership. During their testimonies at a Congressional hearing in December 2023, the presidents of Harvard, MIT, and the University of Pennsylvania were criticized for being "evasive and dismissive" when questioned about whether calls for the genocide of Jews violated university policies on bullying and harassment. Ultimately, it was concluded that these administrators did not condemn such actions.

Instead of denouncing antisemitism and protecting Jewish students, teachers, and pro-Israel advocates, some American high school and college campuses have demonized them, forcing these individuals to barricade themselves in libraries or classrooms for safety.

Jews have been advised to stay in their homes, refrain from wearing their kippot, and avoid speaking Hebrew in public for fear of being targeted.

Jewish people around the world witnessed hate rallies that personally targeted them, their faith, and the nation of Israel. These demonstrations, fueled by pro-Hamas support, have been marked by violence and vocal anti-Israel and anti-Jewish sentiments. As a result, Jews have been advised to stay in their homes, refrain from wearing their kippot, and avoid speaking Hebrew in public for fear of being targeted.

Their only "crime" is being Jewish or expressing support for Israel and the Jewish people. This alarming rise in hostility toward the pro-Israel community clearly illustrates that anti-Zionism is a form of antisemitism.

I am not describing 1938 Nazi Germany — this is today's world, to include America!

Rather than hearing words of comfort following one of the worst assaults in their history, our Jewish friends heard the rallying cry, *"From the River to the Sea — Palestine shall be free."* This well-rehearsed catchphrase is a call for Palestinian control over the entirety of Israel's borders, from the Jordan River to the Mediterranean Sea.

The phrase has been sanitized for English speakers, as in Arabic, it means, *"From the River to the Sea – Palestine Shall be Arab."* Translation: The eradication of the Jewish nation and people.

As opposed to unifying against Hamas' horrific attack on that ill-fated Sabbath morning, many in the international community, the liberal media, and American extremists hurled accusations at Israel, gaslighting the public by dispensing destructive lies about the heinous events of that horrible day.

MARCH FOR ISRAEL

In response to the increased anti-Israel propaganda and as Israel's adversaries became more brazen in their denial of Hamas' atrocities and Israel's right to defend itself, American Zionists responded in force. On November 14, 2023, the largest pro-Israel event in American history occurred in Washington, D.C.

The peaceful gathering comprised nearly 300,000 people from all walks of life, each with diverse opinions on various issues but united by a common purpose: to stand with Israel. The event was awe-inspiring, and I was honored to convey our unconditional support and steadfast defense of the Jewish state and its people.

This pro-Israel event inspired many with hope, yet the lies persisted, and they persist to this day. Pro-Hamas propagandists want the world to believe that America condemns Israel for defending itself and that the Jewish people somehow deserved the despicable deeds executed against them in the October 7 massacre. This destructive agenda is evil, and it must be identified for what it is: demonic hatred against God's covenant nation and people.

> **This destructive agenda is evil, and it must be identified for what it is: demonic hatred against God's covenant nation and people.**

It's concerning to see how deceptive narratives can still gain traction, misleading millions, just as they did with Goebbels, Hitler's propaganda master during WWII. Today, it's vital that we remember the lessons of history and the promise of "NEVER AGAIN." We must stay informed and united to ensure such atrocities are never repeated.

But there is always hope. Recently, a Muslim cleric courageously addressed the core of Jew hatred:

> "The problem the Palestinians have with Israel is not about borders, it's about existence. This we need to realize: if Israel was a Christian state, if it was a communist state, if it was any other state other than the Jewish state, this hatred would not be the way it is. It is the way it is because it's a Jewish state. It's not about feelings, it's about facts, my brother. You have two sides: you have the Palestinians who want to kill the Jews, and you have the Jews, the Israelis, who will not allow them to annihilate their nation. One side wants to kill the other side, and the other side will not allow them to kill their children. It's as simple as that."

Simple but complex, Jew hatred did not begin with the Black Sabbath Massacre, the Holocaust, the Pogroms, the Crusades, or the Inquisition — this revulsion of the Jews is as old as Amalek of the Bible.

CHAPTER 5

Amalek

Among the many evil characters mentioned in Scripture, Amalek, the grandson of Esau, is considered one of the greatest villains. Amalek and the Amalekite nation never accepted the loss of Esau's family birthright and blessing to Jacob. A denial that is at the center of the Jew hatred that exists today.

This animosity caused the Amalekites to wage war against the Jewish people soon after they crossed the Red Sea during their exodus from Egyptian bondage. Because of their malicious and unprovoked attack on the Israelites when they *"were tired and weary"* (Deuteronomy 25:18) and numerous other offenses, God vowed to blot Amalek and his descendants out from under heaven.

> Then the LORD said to Moses, "Write this for a memorial in the book and recount it in the hearing of Joshua, that I will utterly blot out the remembrance of Amalek from under heaven." And Moses built an altar and called its name, The-LORD-Is-My-Banner; for he said, "Because the LORD has sworn: the LORD will have war with Amalek from generation to generation." (Exodus 17:14–16)

Amalek symbolizes the classic archenemy of the Jewish people, and he has had many antisemitic successors. Two of the most vile, Haman and Hitler, planned and attempted to annihilate the whole of the Jewish nation. Even though Amalek, Haman, and Hitler are buried in the boneyard of human history, their spirit lives on through every act of Jewish hatred.

CHAPTER 6

The War Against the Jews

There is no denying it — the world has been at war with the Jewish people since the time God gave them the Torah, the first five books of the Old Testament, on Mount Sinai. Most Christians are unaware of their Hebraic roots, and even more are oblivious to the atrocities committed against the Jewish people in the name of Christ.

Father Edward H. Flannery, in his book *The Anguish of the Jews*, wrote, "The sin of antisemitism

> There is no denying it — the world has been at war with the Jewish people since the time God gave them the Torah.

contains many sins, but in the end, it is a denial of the Christian faith, a failure of Christian hope, and a malady of Christian love."

Bottom line: Christians don't have to hate the Jews in order to love Jesus.[viii]

> King Solomon declares in Proverbs 18:15 that *"The heart of the prudent acquires knowledge, and the ear of the wise seeks knowledge."*

For this purpose, allow me to expand on the root of Jew hatred. Both Biblical accounts and secular history document the unsuccessful attempts made by individuals and nations to eradicate the Jewish people. For centuries, the Jewish community has endured defamation, dispersal, persecution, and systematic annihilation. Despite these relentless efforts to eliminate them, all have ultimately failed.

This all-consuming animosity toward the Jewish people has not been a consequence of their enemy's aims of achieving a political ideal, a necessity to acquire vast resources, or even the objective to confiscate territory — no, this unrivaled hostility exists simply because they are Jews. This one-of-a-kind hatred has been branded anti-Judaism, anti-Zionism, or antisemitism.

CHAPTER 7

Early Antisemitism

Antisemitism is an ancient and sustained crisis of civilization. It is one of the most malicious forms of racism in human history, defined as a despicable fear, hatred, and contempt of the Jewish people and their faith.

This animosity for God's Chosen People has persisted since ancient times and has continued to increase in our modern society. So much so that recently, the International Holocaust Remembrance Alliance — an intergovernmental group comprised of 35 nations — adopted the definition of antisemitism as "a certain perception of Jews, which may be expressed as hatred toward Jews that can also target the State of Israel."[ix]

Early *antisemitism*, first termed *anti-Judaism*, was described as the opposition to the Jewish faith and those who practiced it. At their core, they are one and the same. When Jacob and his sons first entered Egypt to reunite with Joseph, they were the honored guests of Pharaoh Sesostris I, who gave Joseph power over Egypt. However, three generations later, the book of Exodus records examples of Egyptian phobia and scorn toward the Jewish people.

One such example was Thutmose III, the Pharaoh of the Exodus. He singled out the Jewish people for fear they would overtake his reigning government. This persecution set a precedent for the myth that would live through the centuries:

> *Now there arose a new king over Egypt, who did not know Joseph. And he said to his people, "Look, the people of the children of Israel are more and mightier than we; come, let us deal shrewdly with them, lest they multiply, and it happen, in the event of war, that they also join our enemies and fight against us, and so go up out of the land."*
> (Exodus 1:8–10)

After the Exodus from Egypt (1446 BC), Joshua led the Israelites to victory in battles throughout Canaan. Following Joshua's death, Israel was ruled by a series of judges until the prophet Samuel appointed Saul and later David as kings of Israel.

King David conquered the Jebusites and made Jerusalem the capital of Israel. After King David's death, his son Solomon built and dedicated the First Temple in the Holy City (960–953 BC). Following King Solomon's reign, the Northern Kingdom of Israel (10 tribes) broke away from the Southern Kingdom of Judah (two tribes).

Eventually, the Assyrians conquered the Northern Kingdom of Israel, deporting and assimilating the 10 tribes throughout the Assyrian Empire (722 BC). A little over 130 years later, King Nebuchadnezzar conquered the Southern Kingdom, which was comprised of the Tribes of Judah and Benjamin, destroyed the First Temple, and exiled the Jews to Babylon (586 BC). However, throughout their tumultuous history, a remnant of the Jewish people remained in their beloved homeland, Israel.

During their time in exile, the Jewish people experienced assimilation, indoctrination, torture, and death. The Assyrians dispersed the Israelites throughout their vast empire to ensure assimilation, while Nebuchadnezzar allowed them to establish communities within Babylon. As a result, the Jewish people were able to preserve some aspects of their identity and continue their Torah worship traditions.

> **Throughout their tumultuous history, a remnant of the Jewish people remained in their beloved homeland.**

In the first year of his reign, he issued a decree to rebuild the Temple in Jerusalem, allowing Jews who wished to help with the restoration to return to their homeland.

In the 6th century BC, King Cyrus the Great of Persia defeated the Babylonians. During the first year of his reign, the king issued a decree to rebuild the temple in Jerusalem, allowing Jews who wished to help with the restoration to return to their homeland. Although many Jews did return to Jerusalem after Cyrus' Edict, the majority chose to remain in the lands where they had been displaced.

King Xerxes, son of Darius, ruled the Persian Empire from 486 to 465 BC. During this time, Persia encompassed over 127 provinces and included most of the displaced Jews from the Babylonian Exile.

CHAPTER 8

Haman's Final Solution

During King Xerxes' reign, Esther and her cousin Mordecai lived in Shushan, a robust cultural, political, and religious center in Persia. The book of Esther documents the hostility towards the Jews shortly after King Xerxes appointed Haman, the Agagite, as his prime minister.

Haman, a descendant of Amalek, the king of the Amalekites, demanded that the whole kingdom pay him homage. Mordecai refused to bow before Haman lest he offend the God of Abraham. Haman was incensed with Mordecai's defiance, but instead of punishing one man,

> **Mordecai refused to bow before Haman lest he offend the God of Abraham.**

he devised a plan to eradicate the entire Hebrew population from the Persian Empire.

Mordecai's adversary proposed to increase the king's coffers by nearly two-thirds with the spoils he expected to seize from the Jews through his elaborate plot. Haman approached King Xerxes with his lethally deceptive and enticing offer:

> *"There is a certain people* [the Jews] *scattered and dispersed among the people in all the provinces of your kingdom; their laws* [Torah Laws] *are different from all other people's, and they do not keep the king's laws* [dual loyalty]. *Therefore it is not fitting for the king to let them remain. If it pleases the king, let a decree be written that they be destroyed, and I will pay ten thousand talents of silver into the hands of those who do the work, to bring it* [the wealth of the Jews] *into the king's treasuries."* (Esther 3:8–9, additions added)

Professor Rabbi Martin Lockshin states, "On the political level, Haman may have been the first to articulate the 'dual loyalty' argument, contending that the Jews' allegiance to their own laws [the Torah] causes them to be disloyal to the laws of the state."[x]

However, the Lord remained faithful to His promise to Abraham and his descendants in Genesis 12.

Haman, much like Amalek, was a persecutor of the Jews; who sought to exterminate the descendants of Abraham.

However, the Lord remained faithful to His promise to Abraham and his descendants in Genesis 12. Because Persia's prime minister chose to curse the Jews, God saw to it that Haman and his ten sons were hung on the gallows meant for Mordecai.

CHAPTER 9

The Greeks and the Romans

The Persians dominated the Near East and the Mediterranean regions for over two centuries. As one of history's first superpowers, the Persian Empire extended from the borders of India through Egypt and up to the northern borders of Greece. However, its reign ended in 331 BC when Alexander the Great conquered the empire through his military and political genius.

After overtaking the Persian Empire, Alexander and his army marched east and reached as far as India before returning home. But the king of Macedonia did not complete his journey. In 323 BC, at only 32 years of age, he died of a sudden and mysterious illness in the palace of Nebuchadnezzar II in Babylon.

After his death, Alexander's empire was divided into several Hellenistic kingdoms, each governed by one of his generals or their heirs. The most prominent of these kingdoms were:

- The Seleucid Empire in Asia which covered territories from modern-day Turkey to India.

- The Ptolemaic Kingdom in Egypt that included Egypt and parts of the eastern Mediterranean.

- The Antigonid Kingdom in Macedonia controlled the Macedonian and Greek regions.

- The Attalid Kingdom in Anatolia which included the western part of modern-day Turkey.

These kingdoms evolved into independent political entities and continued to influence their respective regions for several centuries.[xi]

With the return of Jewish exiles and the rise of the Roman Empire, the land of Judea was caught between two ruling powers: the Seleucid Kingdom of Syria in the north and Ptolemaic Egypt to the south. These kingdoms, both successors of Alexander the Great's broken empire, were at war with each other for more than a century while the Jewish nation sat at the crossroads.

For much of this period, Judea was seen as a marginal territory. However, when Antiochus IV rose to power around 170 BC, the Jewish people resisted his vision for the new empire, which called for adopting the Hellenistic way of life and the worship of the Greek pantheon, and Antiochus himself declared he was the reincarnation of Zeus.[xii]

While many pagan nations embraced Hellenism, it ignited a cultural civil war in Judea, principally among the high priestly families. According to the books of Maccabees and the Jewish historian Flavius Josephus, Antiochus plundered the Temple in Jerusalem and took the sacred vessels to finance his campaigns during this turmoil.

The Greeks sought to blend their pagan practices with Judaism, challenging the Jews to abandon their faith. Despite these attempts at "de-Judaization," the resilience and steadfastness of the Jewish people prevailed, as the vast majority remained devoted to their cherished beliefs.

Antiochus ordered the plunder of Jewish property and the execution of those who refused to renounce their faith. But ultimately, it

> **The Greeks sought to blend their pagan practices with Judaism, challenging the Jews to abandon their faith.**

was the desecration of the Holy Temple that drove the Jews to revolt.

When the practice of the Mosaic law was prohibited and their temple desecrated, the Jewish people reached a breaking point. Outraged, they united with a priestly family known as the Maccabees. This alliance led to the successful rebellion against Antiochus IV, which ended the oppression of the Jews and allowed for the reconsecration of their defiled Temple in Jerusalem (167–160 BC).

The supernatural victory of the Maccabean Revolt brought a resurgence of Jewish national pride. This sense of liberation generated a wave of Jewish writings declaring the "glories of Israel and envisioned her ultimate triumph over all nations under the scepter of the Messiah."[xiii]

The Jewish people's newfound independence ended when Roman General Pompey captured Jerusalem from the Hasmoneans in 63 BC. Rome adopted the Greek mindset of contempt for the Jewish people, which led to the slaughter of thousands of Jews and the exile of many more.

The Romans were proud of their gods and showed no tolerance for any religion that threatened their beliefs. Despite this, the Jewish people remained steadfast in their commitment to the God of Abraham, Isaac, and Jacob, who prohibited any form of idolatry.

The Greeks and the Romans, like other societies before them, relentlessly targeted the Jewish people because they refused to adapt to their foreign cultures and polytheistic religions. The rejection of their gentile ruler's demands was viewed as a direct rebellion against the established government. Haman's false accusation of "dual loyalty" persisted throughout history.

The Jews who remained in their covenant land and the Jews of the Diaspora, those scattered outside their ancestral homeland, considered Jerusalem to be their Holy City and Jehovah to be their only God.

What the gentile nations failed to understand was that the Jewish people were set apart to God — *by God*. From the time Moses led the Israelites out of Egypt through the moment Joshua led them into the Promised Land, they were cast into "religious and social solidarity."

Edward Flannery describes this cohesion perfectly:

> *"From the heights of Sinai, the voice of Yahweh had thundered forth the tenet of unity: "I, the Lord, am your God...You shall have no other gods before Me...." (Exodus 20:2-3)"; and Israel's election was made no less plain: "I, the Lord, am sacred, I, whom have set you apart from the other nations to be my own.*"[xiv]

CHAPTER 10

The Pharisees, the Sadducees, the Essenes, and Zealots

A brief overview of the four sects of Judaism will clarify how Jewish life was integrated religiously and politically during Roman rule in first-century Jerusalem.

The Pharisees, often regarded as the "spiritual fathers" of modern Judaism, believed in the Torah, or Written Law, and the Oral Law God gave to Moses at Sinai. This Oral Law, which is documented in the Talmud, was compiled about three centuries later. The

Pharisees viewed the Written and Oral Laws as interdependent, and maintained that nothing could supersede the authority of the Written Law.

They believed God revealed the interpretation and application of His laws to Moses. The Pharisees supported the concept of the resurrection of the dead, the existence of an afterlife, God's punishment of the wicked, and His reward of the righteous in the world to come.

They also believed in a Messiah who would bring about an age of world peace. Even after the destruction of their Holy Temple, the Pharisees continued to uphold the principles of Judaism, including individual prayer and communal gatherings in synagogues.

The Sadducees were at the other end of the spectrum as the Pharisees. They believed that God was detached from evil and, as a result, not actively involved in a corrupt world. This "elitist" sect came from priestly, aristocratic, and military backgrounds and was often accused of pursuing wealth and elevated social standing.

The Sadducees accepted Judaism's sacrificial rites but rejected the concept of the Oral Law, insisting on a strict interpretation of the Written Law. They dismissed the belief in an afterlife and primarily concentrated on participating in the rituals associated with the temple.

The Sadducees embraced Hellenism, which refers to ancient Greece's humanistic and classical ideals, and incorporated these values into their everyday lives.

These Greek ideologies emphasized the study of reason and the arts, the pursuit of secular knowledge and civic obligation, the development of the mind and body, and polytheistic worship.

My best friend and fellow Zionist, Rabbi Aryeh Scheinberg, of blessed memory, stated, "In their purest forms, Hellenism and Judaism were opposing forces — the first believed in the holiness of beauty, while the other believed in the beauty of holiness."

While the Sadducees sought influence in high places, the Pharisees believed that it was God's will for them to remain loyal to His Oral and Written Law, no matter who was in power.

Enter the Essenes, a small religious sect that distanced itself from the conflict between the Pharisees and the Sadducees, choosing instead to retreat to desert communities. The Essenes devoted much of their time to studying the Torah and held an even stricter interpretation of the law than the Pharisees. They abstained from temple worship in Jerusalem and were known for voluntarily living in poverty.

The Zealots were the fourth faction to emerge among the Jewish people at the beginning of the first century AD. Unlike the Essenes, who avoided religious and political confrontation, the Zealots actively welcomed it.

These anti-Roman revolutionaries held the fundamental conviction that political and religious liberty from Rome was essential to survival and should be achieved by any means possible. The most recognized account involving the Zealots, aside from leading the revolt against Rome, was their last stand atop the mountain of Masada. The siege of Masada was one of the final events in the First Jewish–Roman War, occurring from 72 to 73 AD. Here, over 900 Zealots took their own lives rather than be captured by the Romans.

During the Second Temple period, Judaism was characterized by these four sects who shared a fundamental faith in the God of Abraham, Isaac, and Jacob, and a commitment to the authority of the Torah as their central religious text. Their strong adherence to their beliefs resulted in significant conflicts with those in power over them.

THE GREAT REVOLT

The Greeks had long Hellenized Jerusalem during their rule, and to complicate matters, the Romanization within parts of the Jewish community eventually replicated a corruption that had previously existed under Antiochus IV Epiphanes.

The local Hellenists and Sadducees were content with their privileged lifestyles and supported Herod, the ruthless and murderous puppet king installed by Rome. In contrast, the average Jewish citizenry deeply despised King Herod for religious and political reasons. The Pharisees, in particular, strongly opposed the contamination of the Jewish faith.

However, even though they contended with the Sadducees' position, they also opposed a Jewish revolt, fearing disastrous consequences. Ultimately, Rome had created a significant divide within Jewish society.

Despite the internal discord among the Jewish religious community, the combination of Rome's financial exploitation through excessive taxation, its blatant hatred for the Jewish people and their faith, and the brazen desecration of their sacred Temple united them. This alliance resulted in the Zealot uprising, known as the Great Revolt, from 66 AD to 70 AD.

The Pharisees saw their worst fears come to pass when the Roman General Titus conquered Jerusalem and its Jewish inhabitants. Josephus documented this brutal and devastating attack that resulted from the Zealot rebellion: "Rome's ruthless and bloody assault on the Jewish people was relentless and ended with the destruction of the Second Temple and the slaughter of over 1,000,000 Jews."[xv]

> **Jews were exiled as captives, slaves, and refugees, with nearly 100,000 taken to Rome to build the Coliseum.**

Following Titus' devastation of Jerusalem, the Jews were exiled as captives, slaves, and refugees, with nearly 100,000 taken to Rome to build the Coliseum under the reign of emperors Vespasian, Titus, and Domitian.

==As foreigners and outcasts in the nations of their scattering, the Jews suffered discriminatory laws, exorbitant taxes, bigoted degradation, and unending cruelty. This hatred became even more intense after the rise of Christianity.==

In addition to the failed uprising and other successive defeats like it, there was a total loss of Jewish political authority in Israel. This forfeiture of sovereignty excluded the Promised Land from being a haven for Jews escaping generational persecution — tragically culminating in the Holocaust.

Despite centuries of exile and oppression, including the emergence of Christianity, the strength and perseverance of God's Chosen People endured overwhelming adversity, once again demonstrating their remarkable resilience and the power of God's covenant promises. The hope for the redemption of the Promised Land remained a central point of their Jewish faith and cherished national identity. This divinely instilled dream finally became a reality in 1948.

CHAPTER 11

The Church Fathers and Judaism

The Jewish people have always maintained an enduring presence in Israel, even after the siege of Jerusalem in 70 AD. Although many were scattered across the ancient world, their unwavering commitment to their faith in whichever nation they were exiled was a powerful testament to their identity in the God of Abraham. Unfortunately, this steadfast devotion faced fierce opposition, especially with the emergence of Christianity within the Roman Empire, which, ironically, led to increased antisemitism.

Initially, followers of Christ were recognized as just another Jewish sect since Jesus and His disciples were all Jewish. For a time, both faiths existed in some semblance of harmony.

Following the Great Commission (Matthew 28:18–20), the apostles began to spread the Gospel to all people through their journeys in Europe and the Middle East. As a result, the number of believers in Christ as their Redeemer rapidly expanded to include non-Jews.

CONSTANTINE AND THE COUNCIL OF NICAEA

The pseudo-conversion of the emperors began with Constantine, who, before a pivotal battle in 312 AD, chose to adopt the Christian faith. However, Constantine's "conversion" was driven by political motives and an ambitious desire for power. The religion he embraced was a corrupt version of Christianity, mingled with pagan beliefs and Hellenistic influences.

Constantine's form of Christianity eventually became the recognized religion of the Roman Empire, taking its place as the official successor to Judaism. In 325 AD, Constantine convened the Council of Nicaea to address various doctrinal debates facing the newly established Roman Church. This gathering was the first of seven councils that brought together church leaders from across the empire. After centuries of persecution led by various Roman emperors, the participants gathered before Constantine, not as enemies but as allies.

Constantine instructed the church leaders to reach a consensus on the key issues dividing them. "Division in the church," he said, "is worse than war." As a result, the previously persecuted religion became state-approved, serving as the spiritual foundation of a society where Christian doctrine governed both public and private life. If Christianity was to function as the Empire's unifying force, it needed to become the sole religion, and its creeds would serve as a means of enforcing doctrinal compliance.[xvi]

By its end, the Council of Nicaea had accomplished two of its primary objectives. The first was to establish a universally accepted definition of Jesus Christ's deity by resolving the controversy of Arianism. This doctrine held that Christ was not divine but a created being. By the end of their gathering, the Council affirmed the orthodox view of Christ as divine and human.

This resulted in the creation of the Nicene Creed, a statement of faith that all Christians were required to believe and practice throughout the Roman Empire as enforced by the state. This creed is still recited in many churches today.

Another argument centered around the observance of Easter. Quartodecimanism, which comes from the Latin *quartus decimus*, meaning 14th, referred to the practice of commemorating Christ's death during Passover, specifically on the 14th of Nisan, as outlined in Leviticus 23:5. This observance could fall on any day of the week, unlike the fixed celebration of Easter, which takes place on the first Sunday following the first full moon after the spring equinox.

Constantine argued for the separation of the Easter observance from the Jewish Passover, clearly stating his position on the matter and his perspective of the Jewish people in a letter written after the First Council of Nicaea ended.

> *"...it appeared an unworthy thing that in the celebration of this most holy feast we should follow the practice of the Jews, who have impiously defiled their hands with enormous sin, and are, therefore, deservedly afflicted with blindness of soul...Let us then have nothing in common with the detestable Jewish crowd; for we have received from our Saviour a different way."* [xvii]

With a pen stroke, the Council formally replaced the God-ordained observance of Passover with the pagan celebration of Easter, which was adapted from the Feast of Ishtar.

> *We also send you the good news of the settlement concerning the holy Pasch, [Passover] namely that in answer to your prayers this question also has been resolved. All the brethren in the East who have hitherto followed the Jewish practice will henceforth observe the custom of the Romans and of yourselves and of all of us who from ancient times have kept Easter [Ishtar] together with you.* [xviii]

TRIUMPHALISM

By 381 AD, Roman Emperor Theodosius I issued an edict, often referred to as Triumphalism, which established Christianity as the only legitimate religion in the Roman Empire. This marked the official end of native cults in the ancient world and led to the formation of the Catholic Church.[xix]

In 396 AD, Theodosius banned the Olympic Games, which were dedicated to the gods, and ordered the destruction of all native temples and shrines or their conversion into churches. During this time, the term "pagans" surfaced as a derogatory label for those who had not yet converted to Christianity.

Theodosius' edict addressed the Jewish people as he updated and codified the original Roman law. The revised edict stated that Jews were allowed to continue attending their synagogues, and their property, including their places of worship, was protected as their communities contributed taxes to the

> **The revised edict stated that Jews were allowed to continue attending their synagogues, and their property, including their places of worship, was protected as their communities contributed taxes to the state.**

state. However, the same revision also decreased social interaction for Jews and limited their economic opportunities. A few examples:

- Proselytizing by Jews was punished by burning at the stake. Jews were forbidden to attack or harass any Jew who became a Christian.

- Jews could not own Christian slaves, which destroyed any competition with Christian enterprises that relied upon slave labor.

- If a Christian converted to Judaism, his property was seized for the treasury.

- Intermarriage between Jews and Christians was prohibited. This was now considered the crime of adultery.

- Jews could no longer have their religious courts but had to bring any actions to the Roman law courts.

- Synagogues were forbidden to use Hebrew as a precaution against conspiracies against the Empire.

- Jews could not work as lawyers or doctors, where intimate details of a person's life could be used against Christians. Jews, pagans, and heretics were forbidden to publicly debate Christian doctrines.[xx]

Despite all the bans, observant Jews continued to adhere to the Torah, God's written law, by faithfully observing the Feasts of the Lord and declining to participate in pagan rituals. Rome's rulers viewed this steadfast loyalty to Judaism as a deliberate defiance of their newly adopted "Christian" faith. This perception escalated when the Jewish people refused to accept Jesus as Lord, per God's command given to Moses, which states, *"Hear, O Israel: The LORD our God, the LORD is one!"* (Deuteronomy 6:4).

SUPERSESSIONISM

Many early church fathers were educated in logic and the principles of rational thought through the teachings of Greek philosophers such as Socrates, Plato, and

Aristotle. Since Judaism and Christianity were rooted in the Old Testament, church leaders like Ignatius, Origen, Martyr, Marcion, and others thought it reasonable to affirm the newly found Christian doctrine by claiming it superseded Judaism. For example, Ignatius, Bishop of Antioch (98–117 AD), stated in his Epistle to the Magnesians:

> *For if we are still practicing Judaism, we admit that we have not received God's favor…it is wrong to talk about Jesus Christ and live like Jews. For Christianity did not believe in Judaism, but Judaism in Christianity.*[xxi]

The concept of Supersessionism, which suggests that the church has replaced the Jews as God's Chosen People due to their rejection of Christ, is still present in some church teachings today. As a result, this unrelenting condemnation of the Jewish people has contributed to the sustained animosity demonstrated against them.

Hatred for the Jews within the Christian movement grew significantly as church leaders like Justin Martyr and others vilified God's Chosen People. In his document, *Dialogue with Trypho*, dated around 160 AD, Martyr stated:

> *"The custom of circumcising the flesh, handed down from Abraham, was given to you as a distinguishing mark, to set you off from other nations and from us Christians. The purpose of this was that you and only you might suffer the afflictions that are now*

justly yours; that only your land be desolated, and your cities ruined by fire, that the fruits of your land be eaten by strangers before your very eyes; that not one of you be permitted to enter your city of Jerusalem. Your circumcision of the flesh is the only mark by which you can certainly be distinguished from other men...as I stated before it was by reason of your sins and the sins of your fathers that, among other precepts, God imposed upon you the observance of the sabbath as a mark."[xxii]

JOHN CHRYSOSTOM

John Chrysostom (349–407 AD), historically known as "The Golden Mouth," occasionally praised the Jews for being God's Chosen People. However, more frequently, he condemned and cursed them, calling them "wretched and miserable" and "good for nothing." Chrysostom continually denigrated the Jewish people especially after they refused to convert to Christianity. An example of his anti-Jewish venom is as follows:

> *Jews are the most worthless of men — they are lecherous, greedy, rapacious — they are perfidious murderers of Christians, they worship the devil, their religion is a sickness....The Jews are the odious assassins of Christ and for killing god there is no expiation, no indulgence, no pardon. Christians may never cease vengeance. The Jews must live in servitude forever. It is incumbent on all Christians to hate the Jews.*[xxiii]

Chrysostom's warped theology was a continued form of anti-Jewish Supersessionism and became the precursor to modern Replacement Theology.[xxiv] His spiteful rhetoric was also intended to discourage Christians from observing the Jewish feasts and customs and prevent them from becoming "sick with a Judaizing disease."[xxv]

Unfortunately, Chrysostom's antisemitic rants and those of other church leaders were used to validate sustained hatred and violence against the Jews. Discrimination against the Jewish people rose significantly throughout the third century, partly due to church fathers' persistent denunciation, such as St. Augustine (354–430 AD), a contemporary of Chrysostom.

In his autobiographical work titled Confessions, Augustine wrote:

> *"How hateful to me are the enemies of your Scripture! How I wish that you would slay them [the Jews] with your two-edged sword, so that there should be none to oppose your word! Gladly would I have them die to themselves and live to you!"*[xxvi]

By the 4th century, Jews were officially marginalized from the societies in which they had lived for generations. They were forbidden to marry Christians or even share meals with them. In Carthage (modern-day Tunisia), Jews were expelled from the region. Entire

Jewish communities across Europe were ravaged by widespread antisemitism.

In Italy and Spain, the Jewish people faced forced conversion or death. Jews were banned from entering Jerusalem, and the Roman Emperor Honorius called for the confiscation of all the gold and silver from the synagogues in the Holy City.

The war against the Jewish people intensified over the next 400 years, from the 5th to the 8th centuries, and was characterized by relentless demonization, denigration, delegitimization, and eventual destruction.

The Theodosian Code, a compilation of laws within the Roman Empire, was ratified in the 5th century under the authority of Eastern Roman Emperor Theodosius II. This code contained provisions that excluded Jews from certain governmental positions and barred them from civil service and all military roles. In 425, Jews were excluded from all remaining public offices, both civilian and military. The Code also reinstated an earlier ban on building new synagogues.[xxvii]

Over time, the Jewish people faced numerous restrictions, including being forbidden from reciting psalms during burial ceremonies and from testifying against

> **The war against the Jewish people intensified over the next 400 years.**

> **Jews were excluded from owning land, holding public office, and pursuing careers as doctors and lawyers.**

Christians in court. Jews were not allowed to join trade guilds, which led to a decline in the number of Jewish craftsmen, such as goldsmiths, silversmiths, diamond cutters, and glassblowers. Furthermore, Jews were excluded from owning land, holding public office, and pursuing careers as doctors and lawyers.

Over time, Muslim caliphs, medieval bishops, and, finally, Nazi organizers mandated the Jews to wear an identifying badge. The Jewish people were set apart from non-Jews by wearing "distinguishing garments" such as the yellow star or the Juden insignia.

In Canon 26 of the Third Lateran Council of 1179, Jews were prohibited from bringing lawsuits against Christians, yet the testimonies of Christians were always accepted against Jews in court proceedings. Jewish people were not allowed to deny inheritance rights to their descendants who converted to Christianity. Additionally, Jews and Muslims were forbidden from employing Christian servants, and the Canon excommunicated any Christian who lived with a Jew or Muslim.

Historian Jules Isaac, a Jewish-French historian focused on the historical roots of antisemitism within Christianity, stated, "After very deep historical research,

I say and maintain that the fate of the Jewish people did not take a truly inhuman character until the 4th century AD with the coming of the Christian empire."

MARTIN LUTHER

After my first trip to Israel in 1978, I realized how little I knew about the Jewish people and Judaism. This insight drove me to undertake a two-year study of the historical relationship between Jews and Christians. I was deeply troubled to discover the roots of anti-Jewish sentiment within the early Church, and I learned that one of the major contributors to this hatred was Martin Luther, the founder of Protestantism.

After the Catholic Reformation of the 16th century, Luther became dejected that the Jews would not convert to his liberating form of Christianity. Because of Luther's unrestrained anger, he authored an evil work entitled *On the Jews and Their Lies* (1543).

In it, Martin Luther asserted that Jews were Christ's killers and demanded their torture and death. Luther stated that the Jews should have their tongues cut out through the backs of their heads, their synagogues burned to the ground, and their children sold into slavery:

> "...set fire to their synagogues or schools and to bury and cover with dirt whatever will not burn, so that no man will ever again see a stone or cinder of them. This

is to be done in honor of our Lord and of Christendom so that God might see that we are Christians..."[xxviii]

In 1935, the Nazis reprinted Martin Luther's inflammatory pamphlet, which later contributed to the horrors of Hitler's Final Solution. Some historians argue that the slanderous attacks by church leaders like John Chrysostom and Luther represented a significant shift from "anti-Judaism" (hostility toward the Jewish religion) to "antisemitism" (hatred toward Jews as a racial group).

JOHN CALVIN

Calvin (1509–1564) was a French theologian and spiritual leader recognized as the most influential ecclesiastical figure in the second generation of the Protestant Reformation. Like some of his predecessors, Calvin held distorted views about the Jewish people, which contributed to the ongoing issues of antisemitism.

> **Like some of his predecessors, Calvin held distorted views about the Jewish people, which contributed to the ongoing issues of antisemitism.**

"I have had much conversation with many Jews: I have never seen either a drop of piety or a grain of truth or ingenuousness — nay, I have never found common sense in any Jew....Their [the Jews] rotten and unbending stiff-neckedness deserves that they be oppressed unendingly and without measure or end and that they die in their misery without the pity of anyone."[xxix]

One undeniable fact is that antisemitism has been present within the church since its inception. The church's defilement and deep-seated hatred of the Jewish people over the centuries is among the ever-present arguments over its contribution to Hitler's attempted extermination of the entire Jewish race during the Holocaust.

> **One undeniable fact is that antisemitism has been present within the church since its inception.**

CHAPTER 12

Crusades, Pogroms, and Ghettos

The Papacy of Leo I (400–461) and the Holy Roman Empire under Charlemagne (800–814) marked a period when the Catholic Church had significant influence over government and daily life across Europe. During this span, Jewish-Christian relations fluctuated, depending on the positions of the current Pope and Holy Roman Emperor.

THE CRUSADES

In the 11th century, Pope Urban II of Rome militarized the church by urging the Christians of Europe to take up the "cross and sword" to liberate the Holy Land from Muslims and take control of Christian holy sites. This call to action initiated the first of eight Crusades, which took place between 1096 and 1291 AD. These violent campaigns elevated the status of European Christians in the region, significantly increasing their influence in the struggle for land in the Middle East.

During the Crusades, participants were promised absolution from their sins when they took up the cause. They were initially instructed to focus their campaigns in the Middle East. However, many Crusaders extended their efforts to target Jewish communities in Europe. During the First Crusade in 1096, Jewish communities faced violent attacks as the Crusaders marched towards Jerusalem, motivated by the slogan, "Why fight Christ's enemies abroad when they are living among us?"

Crusaders believed that they were "fighting in the cause of Christ" when they attacked and killed Jews. Motivated by political, religious, and economic factors, the German Crusade of 1096 resulted in a series of mass murders of Jews committed by mobs of French and German Christians. These vigilantes marched under Christian banners as they moved through Jewish villages, looting, raping, and massacring tens of thousands of Jews on their way to Jerusalem. More Jews were killed in the Rhineland than Muslims died in the Holy Land during this period.

Fundamentally, the seed of Abraham, the cherished and covenant people of God, were slaughtered beneath the Cross of Christ.

THE POGROMS

The dark period of the Crusades led to the rise of "pogroms," which are violent attacks and widespread destruction primarily targeting Jewish communities. Pogrom participants usually organized locally, often with encouragement from government and police officials.

The first recorded pogrom took place in 1241 in Frankfurt, Germany, following a debate about interfaith marriages between Jews and Christians. This tragic event, during which 180 Jews were killed and many others were forced to convert and be baptized, is known as the *Judenschlacht* or the "Slaughter of the Jews."

> **The first recorded pogrom took place in 1241 in Frankfurt, Germany, following a debate about interfaith marriages between Jews and Christians.**

On Easter Sunday in 1389, the Jewish Quarter in Prague was devastated by a vandal-instigated fire, leading to the loss of nearly 1,500 lives.

The term "pogrom" became more used following a series of anti-Jewish riots that occurred in the southern and western provinces of the Russian Empire between 1881 and 1884 after the assassination of Tsar Alexander II. The pogrom leaders committed acts of rape and murder against their Jewish victims, vandalizing and looting their properties.

By now, pogroms were commonplace as a large wave of anti-Jewish riots moved through Russia. During this time, more than 200 anti-Jewish events occurred in Kyiv, Warsaw, and Odesa. The pogroms were vicious; the *New York Times* described the First Kishinev (modern capital city of Moldova) pogrom of Easter 1903 with these words:

> "The anti-Jewish riots in Kishinev, Bessarabia, are worse than the censor will permit to publish. There was a well laid-out plan for the general massacre of Jews on the day following the Orthodox Easter. The mob was led by priests, and the general cry, "Kill the Jews," was taken up all over the city. The Jews were taken wholly unaware and were slaughtered like sheep. The dead number 120 and the injured about 500. The scenes of horror attending this massacre are beyond description. Babies were literally torn to pieces by the frenzied and bloodthirsty mob. The local police made no attempt to check the reign of terror. At sunset the streets were

piled with corpses and wounded. Those who could make their escape fled in terror, and the city is now practically deserted of Jews."[xxx]

Pogroms became so prevalent in subsequent years that historian John Klier noted, "By the twentieth century, the word 'pogrom' had become a generic term in English for all forms of collective violence directed against Jews…"

After the Nazis seized power in Germany in 1933, Adolf Hitler publicly condemned "disorder" and acts of violence. However, in practice, violence against Jews was encouraged. Nazi leaders believed that such violence would help prepare the German population for the harsh antisemitic laws and administrative measures that were later implemented in the name of restoring order.

Kristallnacht, or the Night of Broken Glass of 1938, was the most extensive and most destructive pogrom in Nazi Germany. An unprovoked wave of street violence against the Jewish people manifested in the burning of

> **An unprovoked wave of street violence against the Jewish people manifested in the burning of synagogues, the destruction of Jewish-owned homes and businesses, and physical assaults and unfounded arrests of Jewish people.**

synagogues, the destruction of Jewish-owned homes and businesses, and physical assaults and unfounded arrests of Jewish people.

Kristallnacht, which I will describe in more detail later, was followed by a significant increase in anti-Jewish legislation during the autumn and winter of 1938–1939, which further devastated Jewish communities. During World War II, *Einsatzgruppen*, which were mobile killing units, were commanded to incite the local populations in the newly conquered Soviet territories to carry out anti-Jewish pogroms. These violent riots reflected the German policy of systematically exterminating entire Jewish communities in the Soviet Union.

On June 22, 1941, Nazi Germany and its Axis partner, Romania, invaded the Soviet Union in what was known as Operation Barbarossa. Romanian officials and military units, assisted by German soldiers, killed at least 8,000 Jews during a pogrom in the Romanian province of Moldavia. On July 10, 1941, Polish residents of Jedwabne, a small town located in the Białystok District of first Soviet-occupied and then German-occupied Poland, participated in the murder of hundreds of their Jewish neighbors.

Modern-day pogroms exist today in Russia, Amsterdam, America, and worldwide. But the most hideous is the Black Sabbath attack on Jewish people on October 7, 2023; it was a "pogrom" — a Gazan government-sanctioned attack on the Jewish people of Israel by Hamas.

THE GHETTOS

Throughout the centuries, Jewish communities have faced various forms of discrimination and attacks — politically, economically, religiously, and socially. By the 13th century, many Jews were forced to leave their homes and were relocated to designated areas that eventually became known as "Jewish Ghettos."

> **Many Jews were forced to leave their homes and were relocated to designated areas that eventually became known as "Jewish Ghettos."**

The term "ghetto" originated from the Italian word *gettare*, which means "to cast," as in metal.

It was first used in Venice in 1516 when Italian authorities mandated that Jews relocate to the island of Correggio, referred to as the *Ghetto Nuovo* or the "new ghetto." By the 16th and 17th centuries, Jewish ghettos were established in cities such as Frankfurt, Rome, Prague, and others across Europe.[xxxi]

In Venice, the ghetto was enclosed by a wall, and its gates were locked every night. The Jewish residents of the ghetto were subject to a curfew and were required to wear yellow hats and badges for identification. The

Nazis would later adopt this practice in the territories they occupied. Ghettos in Nazi-occupied Europe are categorized into three types:

Open Ghettos had no fences or walls; however, there were restrictions on who was permitted to leave and return.

Closed Ghettos were surrounded by fences or walls, prohibiting the Jewish people from leaving or entering. The conditions inside these ghettos were extremely unsanitary, with severe shortages of food and water causing high death rates from starvation and disease.

Destruction Ghettos were designated areas in towns and cities that were sealed off for a short period, around two weeks, before the inhabitants were deported to extermination camps.[xxxii]

As the ghettos became more established, the Nazis exploited free labor for the war effort. The Jewish people worked long hours under brutal conditions, and often, the labor served as a form of torture rather than productive work.

For some Jews, work served as a lifeline. Those engaged in forced labor often received additional, though meager, rations and were less likely to be deported. Working outside also provided chances to smuggle extra food or restricted supplies into the ghetto. These opportunities would often prove to be lifesaving, but they also increased the risk of being caught, punished, or even killed.[xxxiii]

By March 1942, the Nazis began deporting the Jewish people from the ghettos as part of Operation Reinhard, the code name for the plan to murder approximately two million Jews living in German-occupied Poland. Under this strategy, three killing centers were established: Bełżec, Sobibor, and Treblinka. These camps used carbon monoxide gas generated by motor engines to execute their innocent victims.

In all, Operation Reinhard murdered approximately 1.7 million Jews in the death camps and through related mass shootings. Those killed also included an unknown number of Poles, Roma (Gypsies), and Soviet prisoners of war.[xxxiv]

> **In all, Operation Reinhard murdered approximately 1.7 million Jews in the death camps and through related mass shootings.**

THE MIDDLE EAST CONFLICT

CHAPTER 13

Myths and Lies

The term "antisemitism" was first introduced by Wilhelm Marr in his 1879 work, *Victory of Judaism over Germanism*. Marr argued that Jews should be denied citizenship due to their alleged conspiracy to dominate the state.

Similarly, Russian writer and mystic Sergei Nilus widely disseminated a fictitious document, titled *The Protocols of the Elders of Zion*, in 1905. Here, Nilus perpetuated the myth that Jews had created a "secret plan to rule the world through economic manipulation, control of the media, and incitement of various religious conflicts."[xxxv]

These writings, considered the "most notorious and widely distributed antisemitic publications of modern times," significantly contributed to the alarming rise in antisemitism. This increase can also be attributed to the emergence of baseless anti-Jewish works, such as Social

Darwinism and other so-called scientific theories that are based on false notions of racial superiority.

This deep-seated hatred has led to unprovoked violence, destruction, persecution, and massacres of Jewish people and communities — before, during, and beyond the Nazi propaganda that so effectively demonized Jews. Ambassador Deborah Lipstadt served as the US special envoy to monitor and combat antisemitism. Ambassador Lipstadt expands on the far-reaching effects of antisemitism:

> "It's imperative that we think of antisemitism as more than just — a threat to the welfare of Jews and the Jewish community…it is more than just that. It's also a threat to democracy.…Antisemitism is free-flowing, moving across every place on the political spectrum. It can come from left, right, center, center left, center right. It can come from Christians, it can come from Muslims, it can come from atheists, it can come from Jews. It is ubiquitous."[xxxvi]

I am reminded of Mordecai's warning to Queen Esther:

"For if you remain completely silent at this time, relief and deliverance will arise for the Jews from another place, but you and your father's house will perish. Yet who knows whether you have come to the kingdom for such a time as this?"
(Esther 4:14)

JEW HATRED BEGINS WITH WORDS

On July 10, 1933, nearly a decade before the Holocaust, Dr. Paul Joseph Goebbels, the Nazi Minister of Propaganda, was featured on the front cover of *Time* Magazine with the banner, "THE JEWS ARE TO BLAME!"[xxxvii] And this headline has followed the Jews since.

However, condemning the Jews began long before the Holocaust and did not end with the murder of six million Jews. It is important to remember that this unprecedented vilification "began with words."

Antisemitism often starts with insensitive remarks that are overlooked or negative stereotypes that go unopposed. Silence, complacency, and indifference in the face of such statements and actions only normalize them.

The current generation's tragic lack of knowledge about what happened to Europe's Jews during World War II makes it hard to recognize and combat antisemitism, especially as Holocaust survivors enter their later years. If we fail to acknowledge the catastrophic reality of the Holocaust, it will fade from memory, allowing Nazism and its horrific actions to appear as mere illusions — and that, my friend, is the goal.

Throughout history, Jews around the globe have faced harmful depictions that have led to their unjust scapegoating, revilement, persecution, expulsion, and murder. Antisemitism portrays Jews as an obstinate opposing force in society, and it relies on age-old lies and propaganda to support its distorted ideology.[xxxviii]

Today, antisemitism has gained newfound acceptance worldwide. Without the willingness to acknowledge this evil, we are hindered in our ability to combat it. The following are a few myths that have followed the Jewish people through the ages.

JEWS SPREAD DISEASE

Throughout history, the Jewish people have faced unjust blame for many of the world's troubles, including the spread of deadly diseases and plagues.

The first significant instance of accusing Jews of spreading diseases occurred in southern France during the 14th century. At that time, Jews, who were less affected by the disease, were blamed for transmitting leprosy to kill Christians. The perception that Jews were less vulnerable to the disease stemmed partly from the hygienic regulations mandated by Jewish law, which included frequent handwashing and ritual baths. This situation led to violent riots, during which both Jews and leprosy patients were murdered.

The disease claimed the lives of 25 million Europeans, roughly 40% of the population.

Jews were unjustly blamed for spreading the virus through common drinking wells, which led to the murder of thousands in retaliation.

This false accusation also resulted in pogroms and the expulsion of entire Jewish communities, including those in Strasbourg in 1349 and Spain in 1492.[xxxix]

When the Bubonic Plague, known as the "Black Death," devastated Europe from 1347 to 1351, the Jews were wrongly accused of poisoning wells to spread the deadly disease. For this and other false allegations related to the plague, nearly 100,000 Jews were burned alive in Germany and Austria alone.[xl]

Following the rise of Nazism, German propagandists wrongly labeled typhus, a lice-spread disease, as a "disease of subhuman, parasitic people," namely the Jews. This baseless claim was used to rationalize the confinement of Jews in ghettos, unfortunately exacerbating the spread of the illness. A prominent theme in the infamous film *Der ewige Jude [The Eternal Jew]* portrayed Jews as disease-ridden rats, highlighting the dangerous misconceptions that fueled even further discrimination.[xli]

More recently, conspiracy theories circulated the internet connecting Jews and Israel with the coronavirus COVID-19. They combined several common antisemitic images, including dirty Jews spreading infection and Jews getting rich by exploiting a defenseless public.[xlii]

BLOOD LIBEL

Since the Middle Ages, the baseless Blood Libel, or "Ritual Murder Charge," has wrongfully accused Jews of committing horrific acts. These malicious myths include the use of Christian blood in Jewish festival rituals and the killing of Christian children to make the unleavened bread eaten during Passover. This longstanding lie is unfortunately tied to the age-old accusation that the Jews are to blame for the death of Jesus Christ.

Additionally, blood libel charges advanced into a widespread accusation of Jews for unrelated murders and other horrific crimes — including the more recent tales of organ harvesting and Zionist Jews killing and eating Palestinian children and drinking their blood.

DEICIDE

Deicide, which promotes the idea that Jews were responsible for the death of Christ, is another deadly myth that has created great suffering for the Jewish people. Antisemites have used this lie to justify their hate, even though historians and theologians overwhelmingly agree that the Jewish people were not to blame for the death of Christ.

For centuries, this myth was spread by early and medieval Christian leaders during their sermons that often inspired church members to seek vengeance for the death of Jesus and to condemn Jews as agents of the devil. The concept of deicide portrayed Jews as resistant to accepting the Gospel because Satan blinded them. Eventually, the Nazis exploited this myth to justify the Holocaust, arguing that the murder of six million Jews was a deserved punishment for their ancestors' role in the death of Jesus.

Diplomat and historian Ambassador Deborah Lipstadt states that these conspiracy myths can be traced

> *Deicide*, which promotes the idea that Jews were responsible for the death of Christ, is another deadly myth that has created great suffering for the Jewish people.

back to the origins of Christianity. According to Lipstadt, the church promoted the belief that "the Jews" conspired to kill Jesus — paving the way for the undermining and marginalization of those who adhered to Judaism.[xliii]

The myth of deicide perpetuates other lies, including the claim that Jews hold excessive power. The logic behind this falsehood implies that if Jews were responsible for the murder of Jesus, they must possess not only great power but also the ability to outsmart God. This myth, along with the fear of excessive Jewish influence, continues today and significantly contributes to the exponential rise of antisemitism.

In 1964, under the leadership of Pope Paul VI, the Catholic Church distanced itself from the Deicide myth with the publication of the "Declaration on the Relation of the Church to Non-Christian Religions" (Nostra Aetate). This document clearly stated that the crucifixion of Jesus "cannot be charged against all the Jews, without distinction, either those living at the time or the Jews of today."

Although many churches have rejected the deicide charge, it sadly still fuels unjustified hatred against the Jewish people. However, the primary testimony refuting Jewish deicide is Jesus Christ Himself when He declared in John 10:18, *"No one takes it away from Me, but I lay it down of Myself. I have power to lay it down, and I have power to take it again. This command I have received from My Father."*

Christ declared that no one could demand His life from Him by law or take it by force; He willingly *laid it down* and took it up again through His resurrection, as was His Father's bidding. Jesus Christ was the "Offeror and the Offering," submitting Himself as a sacrifice for our redemption.[xliv]

The death of Jesus was entirely voluntary. It was part of the divine plan to submit to death and then emerge victoriously alive, according to the command received from God the Father. Jesus not only had the power to lay down His life, but He also had the power to take it up again, in essence, "raising Himself" from the dead.[xlv]

> **Christ declared that no one could demand His life from Him by law or take it by force; He willingly *laid it down* and took it up again through His resurrection, as was His Father's bidding.**

Think of it — God gave Moses the Torah at Mount Sinai, and Jewish hands, inspired by the Holy Spirit, beautifully recorded every word of Scripture. The prophets, the disciples, and the first family of Christianity — all Jewish. Yet these are the very people who have endured the hatred of antisemitism at the hands of self-identified followers of Christ.

WORLD DOMINATION

Another sinister myth is the belief in a Jewish quest for world domination. This claim is based mainly on *The Protocols of the Elders of Zion*, which I mentioned earlier. It suggests that there is a covert plan by Jewish people to take control of the world.

Despite Jews making up only about 0.2% of the global population, this lie claims that this small minority controls significant sectors of society, including banking, media, government, and even the weather.

> Another sinister myth is the belief in a Jewish quest for world domination.

Although the Protocols have been thoroughly discredited as a fraudulent hoax, its accusations continue to circulate among antisemites and are shared both in print and online. The underlying belief perpetuated by this lie suggests that Jews should not hold power, regardless of their values, and that any influence they have poses a threat to the well-being of others.

The irony of this claim lies in the fact that throughout history, the Jewish people have faced persistent discrimination and delegitimization, often lacking control over their destinies, much less external institutions and politics.

HOLOCAUST DENIAL

Many so-called "revisionist historians" claim that Jews either fabricated or distorted the Holocaust to legitimize the establishment of the State of Israel. Some even deny that the Holocaust occurred at all. Holocaust denial refers to any attempt to reject facts regarding the Nazi genocide of European Jews. Both denial and distortion of the Holocaust are forms of antisemitism and Jew hatred.

Today, radical Arab communities continue to teach these and more dangerous lies to their children. They maintain that the Jewish people are the enemies of Allah and that Islam must continue to engage in a religious war against them. Ultimately, this radical Islamic rhetoric teaches that killing Jews is a holy obligation.

The tragic consequences of these diabolical myths, many of which began within the Roman Church thousands of years ago, have advanced sustained hatred against the Jews today, as was witnessed in the October 7 massacre.

Former Israeli Prime Minister Yitzhak Shamir referred to the role of antisemitism in the execution of millions of Jews during the Holocaust. He stated, "[The] Poles "suck it [Jew hatred] in with their mother's milk... This is deeply imbued in their tradition, their mentality."

We must not forget that Jew hatred has no geographical, ethnic, economic, religious, or cultural boundaries — it is an ugly virus that infects all people.

CHAPTER 14

Post-World War I Germany

Germany was humiliated by its defeat in World War I, resulting in the signing of the Treaty of Versailles. This agreement required the German people to relinquish territory and pay reparations to the countries whose lands had been damaged during the war. This situation set the stage for Adolf Hitler's rise.

Hitler was a charismatic leader, which led many Germans to fall into a state of hypnotic obedience to his manipulative authority. He revived the "blood libel" myths, which were falsely associated with the Jewish people, and blamed them for various societal troubles, including the economic decline in Germany.

The German people were crying out for any political and social revolution that would return them to

European dominance and reinstate their lost dignity. To add fuel to the already raging fire, Hitler quoted the works of Chrysostom and Luther to promote fear within the people that the Jews would, in due course, contaminate their "superior Aryan race."

Germany's quest for supremacy allowed Nazism to emerge as a significant political movement. The Nazi Party adopted racially antisemitic ideologies, which Adolf Hitler notably expressed in his book *Mein Kampf* (My Struggle). This book served as Hitler's political manifesto and laid the foundation for National Socialism (Nazism) during Germany's Third Reich.

It was published in two volumes in 1925 and 1927 and a condensed edition in 1930. According to the United States Holocaust Memorial Museum, *Mein Kampf* sold over 12 million copies between 1925 and the end of World War II in 1945, making it a widely distributed book during Hitler's reign.[xlvi]

The demand for the resurgence of German national pride, coupled with existing Jew hatred, culminated in Hitler's meteoric rise to power in 1933. His National

Socialist regime quickly advanced the methodical exclusion of Jews from society from its inception.

The Jewish people were, once again, relentlessly demonized, denigrated, and delegitimized. Ultimately, they were accused of being the driving force behind international Marxism and what Joseph Goebbels called "immoral capitalism." The Jews were the ideal "scapegoat" the Nazis needed to advance their evil agenda. It was a perfect storm — Hitler was even quoted as saying, "If the Jews did not exist, we would have to invent them."

> **The demand for the resurgence of German national pride, coupled with existing Jew hatred, culminated in Hitler's meteoric rise to power in 1933.**

There was no doubt that the ingrained fear and loathing of the Jewish people was the foundation of Hitler's unifying power.[xlvii] He further predicted that if left unchallenged, the Jews would eventually drag their beloved Deutschland into another world war.

Goebbels, Hitler's Minister of Public Enlightenment and Propaganda, and his Nazi machine convinced the German people that the Jews were the root cause of every social, religious, and economic problem they faced. Soon, antisemitic indoctrination saturated German society, contributing to the mass hatred of the Jewish people and the ratification of laws excluding Jews from state and civil service.

The Bavarian Interior Ministry denied Jewish students' entrance to schools and universities. Jewish doctors were forbidden from treating non-Jewish patients, and they were denied reimbursement of services from public or state-supported health insurance funds, thereby leaving them virtually bankrupt.

By 1934, Jewish lawyers and notaries were prohibited from participating in legal matters. Licensing credentials were revoked from Jewish tax advisors; Jewish actors were no longer allowed to perform on stage or screen; and Jewish butchers "could no longer slaughter animals according to ritual purity requirements, effectively preventing them from obeying Jewish dietary laws."[xlviii]

NUREMBERG LAWS

The question arose: who was considered a Jew? Hitler believed that he was the ultimate authority on racial policy, granting him the exclusive power to determine who was classified as Aryan or Jewish. To support Hitler's stance on racial classification, the Nuremberg Laws were enacted. On September 15, 1935, the Reichstag, which was entirely composed of Nazis, passed these decrees during the annual Nazi Party rally in Nuremberg, Germany.

The Nuremberg Laws contained the Reich Citizenship Law and the Law for the Protection of German Blood and Honor. These laws embodied the racial theories underlying Nazi ideology. Now, there was a legal framework in place for the systematic persecution of the Jewish people of Germany.

These antisemitic statutes marked a significant step in clarifying Hitler's "ethnic purity" mandate and consequently removed all Jewish influences from Aryan society. Their said purpose was to protect "German blood and honor" by regulating "the problems of marriage between 'Aryans' and 'non-Aryans.'"[xlix]

Additional Nazi decrees were issued after the Nuremberg Laws that incrementally repealed a Jewish citizen's political, legal, religious, and civil rights. Eventually, these decrees divested the Jewish people of their rights as human beings.

The Reichstag sponsored the use of "racial hygiene" to build their Aryan "master race." And to accomplish their godless plan, it would be necessary to eliminate anyone who did not fit into their racial standards. As a result of this "ethnic cleansing," Hitler demanded the forced sterilization of the Jewish people.

Racial hygiene extremists and morally corrupt doctors would soon merge their inhumane agendas to further the purpose of national socialism. It was a natural fit. Now, the use of corrupt medical science could help achieve Hitler's objective of racial integrity — a fundamental model within the Nazi philosophy.

By 1938, Jews could not legally change their names or the names of their businesses. *The Order for the Disclosure of Jewish Assets* required Jews to report all property over 5,000 Reichsmarks. Additionally, the *Decree on the Confiscation of Jewish Property* directed the transfer of assets from Jews to non-Jewish Germans.

Finally, the Reich's Interior Ministry canceled all German passports held by Jews, with the stipulation that the passport could only be revalidated after the letter "J" was stamped on it. Violating these decrees resulted in strict fines, incarceration, or deportation to labor camps.[1]

The Nuremberg Laws were intentionally designed to provide a legitimate path for the discrimination, persecution, and subsequent extermination of the Jewish people in Germany and throughout their occupied territory.

CHAPTER 15

The Night of Broken Glass

On November 7, 1938, a Jewish young man learned that his family had been deported to Poland after German police had confiscated their life's possessions. Living with an uncle in Paris, the 17 year old became hopelessly distraught and, in retaliation, attempted to assassinate the German ambassador to France. His plan failed, and instead, he fatally wounded an embassy undersecretary.

Joseph Goebbels immediately labeled the attack a conspiracy by "International Jewry." He announced to the German people that the deliberate act was a direct assault on their Führer. This ill-fated incident was all Goebbels needed to instigate retaliation against the

Jewish people throughout Germany, Austria, and other newly acquired Nazi territories.

This sanctioned revenge against the Jewish people produced the infamous *Kristallnacht*, or "Night of Broken Glass," of November 9 and 10, 1938. During these two days, the Nazis burned down over 200 synagogues, destroyed hundreds of Jewish homes, vandalized Jewish day schools, sacked and looted 7,500 Jewish shops, and murdered nearly one hundred Jews throughout Germany and Austria.

In the wake of this terrifying pogrom, some 30,000 Jewish men were arrested and sent to Dachau, Buchenwald, and Sachsenhausen — all established Nazi concentration camps. Before Kristallnacht, the oppressive Nazi policies of sanctioned anti-Jewish boycotts and legislation, as well as staged book burnings, had been painfully hostile; however, after this two-day onslaught, conditions for German and Austrian Jews instantaneously grew much worse.

Within days after *Kristallnacht*, the Nazis issued a decree forcing all Jews to transfer their businesses to Aryan hands. Jewish students were expelled from all German schools, and the government levied a collective one billion Reichsmark ($400,000,000) "penalty" against German Jews for the destruction of property during this reprehensible "Night of Broken Glass."[li]

Goebbels convinced Germany that they had a widespread "Jewish problem."

A few months after *Kristallnacht,* Hitler delivered his infamous speech to the Reichstag in celebration of the sixth anniversary of his ascent to power. Now Führer and Reich Chancellor, Hitler made a self-fulfilling prophecy regarding the future of the Jewish people:

> "Today I will once more be a prophet: If the international Jewish financiers in and outside Europe should succeed in plunging the nations once more into a world war, then the result will not be the Bolshevization of the earth, and thus the victory of Jewry, but the annihilation of the Jewish race in Europe!"[lii]

Before his speech, Hitler's Third Reich took part in ongoing negotiations with the Intergovernmental Committee on Refugees regarding the complete emigration (relocation) of Jews from Germany to the nations of the world.

There was a "Catch 22," however; the potential recipient nations did not want the Jews without their wealth, and the Reich was not willing to allow them to leave with any of their possessions, which they believed rightfully belonged to Germany.[liii]

There was no solution in sight; the gates of escape were closing.

CHAPTER 16

The Undesirables

After Hitler's Reichstag speech, Jewish people became "persona non grata" throughout Europe. A clear example of their rejection worldwide is the ill-fated voyage of the St. Louis.

In the early 1930s, many Jewish families recognized the looming danger and voluntarily emigrated from Europe to various countries, including America. However, many more chose to stay behind. After *Kristallnacht*, the situation for Jews grew much worse — those who could sought asylum in the West as a means of personal survival.

On May 13, 1939, 937 Jewish passengers boarded the St. Louis, a German transatlantic liner, in Hamburg, bound for Havana. For many of these passengers, this voyage represented their last hope to escape the horrors of Nazism.

Every traveler took great pains to meet the strict immigration laws, which included increased levies, overpriced visas, and often mandatory sponsorship. The passengers of the St. Louis had secured travel vouchers and required visas; however, most of their documentation was invalid when they arrived off the coast of Cuba.

The Cuban people were concerned about the rising influx of migrants into their country, believing this increase was directly causing the lack of jobs, further impacting their struggling economy.

Seizing on this situation, Goebbels dispatched SS agents to Havana, aiming to stir animosity toward Jewish immigrants by employing his familiar, deceptive tactics that had previously succeeded in Europe. He labeled the passengers of this ill-fated journey as "undesirables," portraying them as threats to the welfare of Cuba.

When the St. Louis arrived in Havana harbor on May 27, the Cuban government permitted only 28 passengers with valid visas to enter. Additionally, one passenger was taken to a hospital in Cuba after attempting suicide. The remaining 908 passengers were denied entry.

On June 2, the ship was forced to leave Cuban waters. In desperation, international Jewish groups sought a country that would accept the refugees, but within two days, every government in Latin America refused the desperate passengers. By now, the plight of the St. Louis gained international attention. Although several countries sent telegrams of protest to the Cuban government, no nation was willing to offer asylum to the Jews, including the United States.

While negotiations with other nations were ongoing, the St. Louis sailed around Cuba and eventually reached the coastline of Miami, hoping that America would accept the refugees. However, the U.S. Coast Guard prevented the ship from coming closer. On June 7, 1939, the captain had no choice but to return the St. Louis and its "forbidden cargo" to Germany. In response to this injustice, a resident of Virginia wrote:

> "[The] press reported that the ship came close enough to Miami for the refugees to see the lights of the city…the U.S. Coast Guard, under instructions from Washington, followed the ship…to prevent any people landing on our shores…this horrible tragedy was being enacted right at our doors, our government…made no effort to relieve the desperate situation of these people, but on the contrary gave orders that they be kept out of the country…The failure to take any steps whatsoever

to assist these distressed, persecuted Jews in their hour of extremity was one of the most disgraceful things which has happened in American history and leaves a stain and brand of shame upon the record of our nation."[liv]

The denial of refuge for the passengers of the St. Louis presented the Nazis with an ideal opportunity to legitimize their anti-Jewish objectives and policies aimed at forced emigration. Joseph Goebbels effectively transformed the situation into a global propaganda victory, arguing that it demonstrated that Jews were universally despised, mistrusted, and unwanted.

Due to God's intervention and exceptional negotiations, the American Jewish Joint Distribution Committee (JDC) identified several countries willing to accept the refugees.

Thirty-six emotionally charged days later, the ship was allowed to dock at Antwerp, Belgium, on June 17, with the remaining passengers; 181 went to Holland, 224 to France, 228 to Great Britain, and 214 to Belgium.[lv] America accepted none. Of the original 937 passengers that boarded the St. Louis, approximately 709 survived the war, and 228 did not.[lvi]

The brave children aboard the St. Louis poured their hearts into letters to First Lady Eleanor Roosevelt, pleading for refuge. Meanwhile, the adult passengers sent a heartfelt telegram to President Roosevelt, urgently asking for help: "Most urgently repeat plea for help for the passengers of the St. Louis. Mr. President, help the nine hundred passengers, including over four hundred women and children."

Their cries for help went unanswered.

Joseph Loeb, who traveled on the St. Louis as a child, recalled the passengers' despair:

> "At the time, we were in the harbor of Havana, and things just weren't moving along. We had some suicide attempts, and there was near panic on board because… many of the men all had to sign they would never return to Germany and if we had returned to Germany, the only place where we would have ended up was in a concentration camp because we had no homes left. We had no money left and we had nothing left…*The world just didn't care.*"[lvii]

The voyage of the St. Louis revealed the disturbing disregard for God's Chosen People. Were 937 law-abiding asylum seekers a threat, or was this another ill-fated display of indifference?

CHAPTER 17

World War II

The years between the First and Second World Wars were marked by significant international instability. In 1920, two years after the end of World War I, President Woodrow Wilson established the League of Nations, a global organization designed to manage future conflicts between countries and promote world peace.

The League of Nations proved ineffective when it failed to respond to Japan's invasion of Manchuria in 1931. This inability to act contributed to a resurgence of turmoil among global powers. Additionally, the financial devastation caused by the Great Depression in America in 1929 plunged the world into a deep recession.

When Hitler rose to power in 1933, he exploited the global economic disaster and the German people's deep resentment of the Treaty of Versailles to assert that his country required more *Lebensraum*, or living space.

As a result, in 1936, Hitler remilitarized the Rhineland, which was a direct violation of the Treaty of Versailles.[lviii] During this same period, Prime Minister Benito Mussolini elected to follow Hitler's example by conquering territory he thought rightfully belonged to Italy.

Ignoring protests from the League of Nations, Mussolini declared a new Italian empire in East Africa by invading and colonizing Ethiopia and the pre-existing territories of Italian Somaliland and Eritrea. Mussolini believed this forced annexation would create more job opportunities for unemployed Italians and acquire more mineral resources, driving back the effects of the world economic depression.[lix]

Hitler's and Mussolini's blatant and unchecked violations highlighted the incompetence of the League of Nations. Nazi Germany aimed to conquer and expand through the systematic colonization of Europe, while Mussolini sought to recreate the Roman Empire by seizing parts of the Mediterranean and Africa. This shared ambition brought both dictators into an

> **Hitler's and Mussolini's blatant and unchecked violations highlighted the incompetence of the League of Nations.**

alliance, with no effective opposition to stop their aggressive actions.

The situation became even more complex when Japan entered the mix. The Japanese felt a deep resentment toward America's refusal to recognize their "Racial Equality Clause" in the League of Nations covenants. This rejection and the League's ineffectiveness in asserting its authority over Germany and Italy contributed to Japan's alienation from the West.

In 1937, Japan declared war on China to address its escalating economic issues. The United States opposed Japan's aggression by imposing trade embargoes and economic sanctions. Japan relied on imports for over 90% of its fuel, and the U.S. oil embargo proved the final tipping point.

The world was once again on the brink of war. In late August 1939, just days before the outbreak of World War II, Hitler and Stalin signed the German-Soviet Non-Aggression Pact, also known as the Molotov-Ribbentrop Pact. Through this agreement, Germany and the Soviet Union divided their occupied territories between them and pledged not to attack each other.

Things began to progress rapidly; one week after the Non-Aggression Pact was signed, Hitler invaded Poland on September 1. In response to the invasion, France and Great Britain declared war on Germany on September 3, 1939.

By the summer of 1940, Italy had allied with Germany and its Axis Powers, which included nations aligned with Germany. The Nazis continued their advances through Europe and the Mediterranean. As intended, Hitler broke his promise to Stalin and focused on the Soviet Union. However, due to a major offensive, the Soviet Union prevented Germany from entering Moscow. After Hitler's betrayal, Stalin emerged as a key player within the Allied Powers, which opposed Germany.

America did everything possible to avoid involvement in the war in Europe. However, when Japan attacked Pearl Harbor on December 7, 1941, Congress declared war on Japan the following day. Just four days later, on December 11, Germany and Italy declared war on the United States.

Once the lines were drawn, and the combatants were identified as the Axis and Allied powers. The Axis nations included Nazi Germany, Fascist Italy, and Imperial Japan. The Allied nations comprised the Constitutional Monarchy of Great Britain, the Communist

States of the Soviet Union, and the Democratic United States of America.

World War II began in the fall of 1939 and ended in 1945. This unprecedented conflict involved nearly every major nation on earth. For 2,190 consecutive days, an average of 27,000 people were killed every day, making World War II the most devastating conflict in human history.

However, few in the world knew that Hitler was conducting his *secret war against the Jews* within the confines of his conquered territory. By the end of the war, the Nazis would be directly responsible for murdering two-thirds of the Jewish population of Europe.[lx]

> **Few in the world knew that Hitler was conducting his *secret war against the Jews* within the confines of his conquered territory.**

CHAPTER 18

Hitler's Final Solution

From 1938 to 1942, the Jewish people of Europe endured countless pogroms, forced relocations into cramped and disease-infested ghettos, and, finally, compulsory deportations to concentration camps. God's Chosen People suffered unspeakable humiliation, denigration, persecution, and torture.

> Under the Reich's rule, the Jewish people had lost their homes and life possessions, their rights as German citizens, and, in due course, their existence as part of the human race.

Several contributing factors ultimately influenced the evolution of "Nazi racial antisemitism into Jewish genocide."

Among the major influences were:

- Hitler's never-ending lies depicting the Jews as an inferior race.

- The incessant portrayal of the Jewish people as "communist subversives, war profiteers, and hoarders."

- The false Nazi propaganda of the Jewish agenda to gain world dominance at the expense of German Aryans.

- The Nuremberg Laws.

- Violent pogroms such as *Kristallnacht*.

- The massive complications arising from overcrowded, disease-infested Jewish ghettos and concentration camps.

- The Wannsee Conference.[lxi]

THE WANNSEE CONFERENCE

In January 1942, Hitler delegated Reinhard Heydrich to devise and implement a comprehensive plan for the "final solution." Heydrich, second in command of the SS, convened the Wannsee Conference in Berlin. Here, he gathered 15 top Nazi officials to coordinate a systematic plan to exterminate the entire Jewish population of Europe, which was estimated to be about 11 million people.

Every Jewish man, woman, and child in Europe and North Africa was tagged for annihilation. Eventually, 6 million Jews, including 2 million children, were murdered by the Nazis between 1942 and 1945.

This atrocious act of genocide is called the Holocaust. To carry out their grisly plan, the Nazis transported Jews to "purpose-built extermination camps." Once there, the Jewish captives were systematically murdered in gas chambers and incinerated in crematoriums. By the time the war was over, a total of six killing centers and thousands of concentration camps existed in Germany and its Nazi-occupied territory.[lxii]

> **Eventually, 6 million people, including 2 million children, were murdered by the Nazis between 1942 and 1945.**

CHAPTER 19

The Silent Church

Isaiah 33:6 states, *"Wisdom and knowledge will be the stability of your times, and the strength of salvation; the fear of the LORD is His treasure."*

While it is impossible to fully convey the horrors of the Holocaust, several credible books and firsthand testimonies document the atrocities committed against the Jewish people. Christians must recognize the hateful crimes perpetrated against God's Chosen People in the name of Supersessionism, Replacement Theology, and ultimately, in the name of Jesus Christ.

> Understanding this history helps us comprehend the Jewish response to our unconditional offer of friendship and steadfast support — something they have often not experienced in the past.

We ask, "How could this happen?" How could the Nazis murder over 6 million Jewish people in cold blood while the world stood idly by? Why did most Christians ignore this deliberate massacre? How is it that those who shared God's Torah with us, who brought forth the patriarchs, who gave us the apostles, and most importantly, our Redeemer, be so despised? Why was the church silent?

While the church, as a whole, was silent in the defense of the Jewish people, it was not silent in condemning them.

Holocaust historian Raul Hilberg described how antisemitism within the church created the perfect environment for Hitler's final solution to the Jewish problem:

"The missionaries of Christianity had said in effect: You have no right to live among us as Jews. The secular rulers who followed had proclaimed: You have no right to live among us. The German Nazis at last decreed: You have no right to live."[lxiii]

The suffering endured by the Jewish people cannot be attributed solely to Hitler and his followers. The Nazis received active assistance and cooperation from professionals in various fields, many of whom were not members of the Nazi Party. Additionally, church leaders, who could affect public opinion, remained largely silent in the face of the harassment and oppression of the Jews.

In truth, most Christian leaders in Germany supported the rise of Nazism in 1933. The attitudes and actions of German Catholics and Protestants regarding the Nazis' treatment of the Jews were often shaped by their political and social perspective and by the deep-seated antisemitism that existed within their Christian traditions.

There were several reasons why most Christian leaders in Germany accepted the rise of Nazism. Some feared government reprisal if they openly denounced the Nazis' treatment of the Jews, leading to severe consequences for the church and its members, including potential arrests and executions. The Vatican also hoped to maintain diplomatic relations with the Nazi regime, leading to a cautious approach regarding public criticism.

Even others were persuaded by the statement on "Positive Christianity" of the 1920 Nazi Party Platform, which read:

> "We demand the freedom of all religious confessions in the state insofar as they do not jeopardize the state's existence or conflict with the manners and moral sentiments of the Germanic race. The Party, as such,

> **Church leaders, who could affect public opinion, remained largely silent in the face of the harassment and oppression of the Jews.**

upholds the point of view of a positive Christianity without tying itself confessionally to any one confession. It combats the Jewish-materialistic spirit at home and abroad and is convinced that a permanent recovery of our people can only be achieved from within on the basis of the common good before individual good."[lxiv]

Despite the evident antisemitism in this statement, many Germans perceived it as a reaffirmation of Christian values. It is essential to acknowledge that by choosing to remain silent in the face of evil, Christian leaders became complicit in the persecution and eventual murder of millions of Jews alongside other Germans. This complicity was also contagious, spreading to non-Jewish citizens in the conquered territories of Europe.

It is important to note that while the church as an institution did not publicly denounce the Holocaust, some individual clergy, church organizations, and Christian men and women secretly provided shelter and life-saving assistance to the Jewish people at the risk of their own safety. These courageous people are known as the Righteous Among the Nations.

CHAPTER 20

The Sin of Indifference

The question arises, "Why didn't America do more to intervene with the evils of the Holocaust?"

During the war, the Allied Nations, including the U.S., prioritized achieving victory over their enemies more than humanitarian issues. As a result, addressing the plight of the Jews facing Hitler's final solution was not viewed as a top concern.

Factors such as widespread American antisemitic sentiments and domestic issues, including unemployment and national security, meant that very little attention was given to the suffering of European Jews.

Even though history records the actions of several Jewish organizations and a few righteous gentiles throughout the world who bravely confronted the evils of antisemitism — most of the world's citizens were apathetically silent.

My friend and Holocaust survivor, Elie Wiesel, provided a sobering and thought-provoking answer to this insightful question:

> *At best, America was indifferent. The opposite of love is not hate; it's indifference. The opposite of beauty is not ugliness; it's indifference. The opposite of faith is not heresy; it's indifference. And the opposite of life is not death but indifference between life and death.*[lxv]

CHAPTER 21

One Man Had Two Sons

The most pressing geopolitical crisis of our time is the Arab-Israeli clash over who owns the Promised Land of Israel. Where did this dispute begin? The quarrel between the Jews and Arabs first occurred after Abram took Hagar as his concubine at the urging of his wife Sarai.

Hagar conceived Ishmael, and soon after, Hagar and Sarai despised each other (Genesis 16:5–6). The deep resentment between the two women grew even greater when Isaac, the son of promise, was born to Abraham and Sarah. This generational conflict is part of the root cause of Jew hatred for Abraham's descendants to this day.

Some Arabs believe that the Promised Land belongs to them because they, too, are the seed of Abraham. The Arab nations indeed have Abraham as their father through Ishmael. Abraham loved his firstborn and wanted him to be included in the covenant, pleading to God, *"Oh, that Ishmael might live before You!"* (Genesis 17:18).

The Lord God of Israel answers Abraham's plea in Genesis 17:19:

> Then God said: "No, Sarah your wife shall bear you a son, and you shall call his name Isaac; I will establish My covenant with him for an **everlasting covenant**, and with his descendants after him."

Genesis 17:20–21 refers specifically to Ishmael:

> "And as for Ishmael, I have heard you. Behold, I have blessed him, and will make him fruitful, and will multiply him exceedingly. He shall beget twelve princes, and I will make him a great nation. But My covenant I will establish **with Isaac**, whom Sarah shall bear to you at this set time next year."

Paul later restated God's position in Galatians 4:28–31. Fast forward to the 21st century, and God Almighty fulfilled His promise to Abraham when the twelve princes of Ishmael came together as the OPEC nations, creating one of the wealthiest conglomerates on planet Earth.

The world's most heated issue in the Middle East, which has divided men and nations, can be explained in two simple sentences: *One man had two sons. One inherited The Land, and the other inherited the oil.*

CHAPTER 22

The Title Deed

Historic Christian anti-Judaism and European antisemitism produced massive horrors such as the Great Inquisition, the Russian pogroms, and Hitler's Final Solution. However, in the Middle East, the continual struggle for control of the Holy Land of Israel has been stained with Jewish blood for centuries.

Throughout the past 3,000 years, many of the world's greatest civilizations have tried to control Jerusalem. However, only one group of people has been granted the divine right to claim it as their eternal inheritance: the Jews. Because the Jewish people have steadfastly refused to give up this claim, they have endured a tremendous cost in terms of suffering and bloodshed.

Even in the first century AD, after the Romans destroyed Jerusalem, killed over one million of its inhabitants, and exiled hundreds of thousands more, a small remnant of the Jewish people remained in their Biblical homeland.

While many of their fellow Jews suffered in the global diaspora, this remnant remained in Israel since Joshua led them into their God-given inheritance nearly 4,000 years ago. The Jewish people of Israel were oppressed by a succession of brutal and merciless overlords, yet they continued to serve as caretakers of their ancestral homeland, which is deeply interwoven with their faith.

THE ABRAHAMIC COVENANT

> **Understanding the Abrahamic covenant gives a comprehensive understanding of the Bible.**

Understanding the Abrahamic covenant gives a comprehensive understanding of the Bible. It marks the first recorded instance of God speaking directly to Abraham. Christian theologian John Walvoord noted:

> "It is recognized by all serious students of the Bible that the covenant with Abraham is one of the important and determinative revelations of Scripture. It furnishes the key to the entire Old Testament and reaches for its fulfillment into the New. The analysis of its provisions and the character of their fulfillment set the mold for the entire body of scriptural truth."[lxvi]

THE GENESIS 12 PROMISE

After Abram responded to the Lord's call to separate himself from his idolatrous past, country, and family, God made a covenant with him in Genesis 12:1–3.

This promise included four provisions:

1. God will give land to Abram and his descendants (v. 12:1; Hebrews 11:8–9).

2. God will make Abram's descendants into a great nation (v. 2).

3. God will make Abram's name great (v. 2).

4. God will bless those who bless Abram and curse those who curse him (v. 3).

Once Abram arrived in Canaan, God expanded His promise in Genesis 13:14–17:

5. God, the owner of the Earth, will give Abram all the land he can see (v. 15).

6. Abram's descendants will become as numerous as the dust of the earth (v. 16).

God ratifies His unconditional and irrevocable covenant in Genesis 15:5–21:

7. God Himself offered a blood sacrifice and sealed the Abrahamic covenant (v. 17).

In Scripture, there are two types of covenants: conditional and unconditional. A conditional covenant is a mutually binding agreement between two parties. It typically includes a stipulation, expressed as *"if you will, then I will."*

A person's compliance or failure to uphold their part of an agreement can lead to either positive outcomes or negative consequences. A clear example of a conditional covenant is God's agreement with Adam in the garden of Eden, as described in Genesis 2:15–17.

An unconditional covenant is a sovereign act of God made possible by His unmerited grace. It is a one-sided promise that relies entirely on God's integrity for its fulfillment. In this type of covenant, God fully commits Himself to provide specific blessings and conditions for the people with whom He has established the covenant.

The promises in Genesis 12:1–3 represent a covenant defined by God's commitment reflected in His use of *"I will."* This phrase emphasizes His determination to fulfill His promises. While there may be specific conditions that God asks the participant to meet within the covenant, these do not change its unconditional nature nor serve as the basis for God's fulfillment of His promised blessings.

> **While there may be specific conditions that God asks the participant to meet within the covenant, these do not change its unconditional nature nor serve as the basis for God's fulfillment of His promised blessings.**

The Abrahamic covenant involved animal sacrifices and the symbolic passing between the split pieces of the animals. This enactment represents the irrevocable nature of the agreement.

In Genesis 15:18–21:

- God specifies the exact borders of the Royal Land Grant.

In Genesis 17:7–8:

- God refers to the Abrahamic covenant as My covenant (v. 7).

- God underscores His eternal covenant extending to Abraham's descendants (v. 7).

- God calls His covenant an everlasting covenant (v. 7).

- God promises to be the God of Abraham and his descendants forever (v. 8).

The Abrahamic covenant is reaffirmed in Genesis 22:15–18, which addresses the Promised Land, Abraham's descendants, and Israel as a blessing to the world's nations.

The same covenant was also made with Isaac and his descendants as an everlasting promise (Genesis 17:19–21). Currently, the nation of Israel occupies only a minuscule portion of the land that God promised in the Abrahamic covenant. The complete fulfillment of this promise will take place during the millennial reign.

The Abrahamic covenant is reaffirmed in Genesis

22:15–18, which addresses the Promised Land, Abraham's descendants, and Israel as a blessing to the world's nations. God also confirms this covenant to Jacob in Genesis 28:13–22. Further references to the covenant can be found in 1 Chronicles 16:15–22, Psalm 105:7–12, and Hebrews 6:13–18.

God owns the earth as Creator of the universe, and He deeded the land of Israel to Abraham and his descendants through a blood covenant. These Scriptures emphasize that the Abrahamic covenant was established by God Himself, making it inherently self-reliant, unalterable, and irrevocable.

CHAPTER 23

The Jewish State

The Jewish people, who were scattered among the nations by the Assyrians, Babylonians, and Romans, faced hostility and bigotry in their host countries for centuries. Many came to understand that the only way to escape persistent antisemitism and its deadly consequences was to regain their national independence.

In the late 19th and early 20th centuries, after nearly two millennia of exile, God began calling His people home. In 1896, Theodor Herzl published his Zionist pamphlet, *Der Judenstaat* (The Jewish State), which sparked a new hope for Jewish sovereignty.

THE JEWISH QUESTION

Herzl outlined a vision that ultimately led to the re-establishment of the State of Israel. He presented his solution to the "Jewish Question," a historical debate in the 19th and 20th centuries concerning the status and treatment of Jews within European society.

This debate centered on the Jewish people's civil, legal, and political rights and their degree of assimilation into different segments of society. This so-called question was frequently manipulated by antisemitic movements and ultimately culminated in the Nazi regime's "Final Solution to the Jewish Question," a plan for the systematic extermination of Jews during the Holocaust.

Herzl's dream gained worldwide support:

"I believe that I understand antisemitism, which is really a highly complex movement. I consider it from a Jewish standpoint, yet without fear or hatred...I think the Jewish question is no more a social than a religious one...It is a national question, which can only be solved by making it a political world question to be discussed and settled by the civilized nations of the world in council. We are a people — one people. We want to lay the foundation stone, for the house which will become the refuge of the Jewish nation. Zionism is the return to Judaism even before the return to the land of Israel."[lxvii]

The concept of Zionism, the belief that the Jewish people had a right to national independence and sovereignty as natives of their ancestral homeland, began to grow.

JUDEA

In 132 AD, Simon bar Kokhba initiated a revolt against the Romans who occupied Judea. For nearly three years, Bar Kokhba successfully led a Jewish state. However, the Romans ultimately killed him at his last stronghold in Betar, a town in the Judean hills. Following his death, the Romans killed or enslaved Bar Kokhba's followers and executed Rabbi Akiva ben-Joseph, who is referred to in Jewish writings as the "Chief of the Sages."

To add insult to the already devastating injuries, the Romans, in retaliation to the revolt, renamed Judea after the ancient Philistines, Israel's historic adversaries, giving rise to the term "Palestine." This land, primarily located around today's Gaza Strip, has a significant background. Remember, it was David, the future king of Israel, who triumphed over the Philistine giant Goliath with just a sling and five smooth stones — a powerful reminder of the strength and resilience of the Jewish people in the face of conflict.

No matter the historical truth, most of the world continues to use the name "Palestine," a term given by foreign invaders, rather than honoring Israel's rich Biblical heritage as the indigenous land of the Jewish people.

In response to Herzl's passionate call to return to Judea, their homeland, Jewish immigrants eagerly began arriving in "Palestine." Eventually, they purchased land from wealthy Arab landowners at exorbitant prices. Although much of the land had been barren and sparsely populated for years, it held significant value for the Jewish people, who viewed it as a divinely ordained opportunity to return home.

Palestine began to thrive as Jewish returnees cultivated the land, eliminated disease-infested swamps, and improved the area's standard of living and economic opportunities. A miracle was unfolding — the Arab population grew and flourished alongside their Jewish neighbors, and for a season, the two communities peacefully coexisted.

CHAPTER 24

100 Years of Terror

Amin al-Husseini was an Arab nationalist who played a major role in the Palestinian Arab resistance to Zionism. In 1921, the British appointed Husseini the Grand Mufti of Jerusalem and the president of the newly established Supreme Muslim Council, which became the most authoritative religious body in the Palestinian Muslim community.

In this position, Husseini held authority over the Muslim holy sites, establishing him as both the spiritual and political leader of the Palestinian Arabs, who were resolutely opposed to the Jewish presence in the region. To assert their political ends, the radical Arab nationalists turned to terrorism as a means of igniting an era of violence toward the Jews.

As Mufti, Husseini continued to incite resentment and violence against the Jewish community. Worried that Zionism was gaining international financial backing, Husseini spread a rumor of a Zionist plot to seize control of the Muslim holy sites, which successfully fueled further riots. Before long, suicide squads, in defiance of the international accord aimed at reinstating a Jewish state, began targeting local Jews.[lxviii]

Husseini's lies worked. British authorities uprooted Jewish families from their ancestral homes in Hebron and Gaza. They severely restricted Jewish immigration to Palestine and drastically reduced the size of the land intended for a Jewish state. Despite the extreme concessions made by the British, none were able to satisfy the Arab leaders.

To further aggravate the situation, the Mufti traveled to Germany during World War II and met with Adolf Hitler. The Führer's deep-seated hatred for the Jews and his plans for their annihilation resonated with Husseini, who collaborated with the Nazi regime to recruit tens of thousands of Muslims for the SS.

> **British authorities uprooted Jewish families from their ancestral homes in Hebron and Gaza. They severely restricted Jewish immigration to Palestine and drastically reduced the size of the land intended for a Jewish state.**

After the war, Amin al-Husseini was forced to flee Jerusalem to escape prosecution for war crimes and lived abroad for the remainder of his life. Despite this, Husseini's dark legacy of terrorism became a powerful propaganda tool against the Jewish state and people, serving as a model for future despots throughout the last century.

CHAPTER 25

The Balfour Declaration

After Britain and the Allied Powers defeated the Ottoman Turks during World War I, the Middle Eastern Empire was divided into territories later designated for future states. In 1917, British Foreign Secretary Arthur James Balfour wrote a letter known as the Balfour Declaration, in which he expressed British support for re-establishing a Jewish homeland in Palestine. This led to international recognition of the Jewish people's undeniable right to sovereignty in their ancestral homeland.

The Balfour Declaration was a crucial document as it recognized the historical rights of the Jewish people to their national homeland. The declaration stated:

> "Whereas recognition has thereby been given to the historical connection of the Jewish people with Palestine and to the grounds for reconstituting their national home in that country."

BRITISH MANDATE FOR PALESTINE

On May 24, 1922, the League of Nations, the predecessor to the United Nations, entrusted Great Britain with implementing the Balfour Declaration through the British Mandate of Palestine.

The legally binding mandate acknowledged the "historic connection of the Jewish people" to the region, correctly referred to as the Land of Israel, Judea, or the Holy Land.[lxix] It is important to note that the Balfour Declaration and the British Mandate did not establish Jewish historical rights but *recognized an existing right*.

The bloody Arab riots of the 1920s and 1930s convinced the British that the promises made to God's people might not be worth the trouble. Zionism also faced opposition from the British officers responsible for administering Britain's Mandate in Palestine.

These officers took significant measures to make life difficult for the Jewish people, who were prohibited from owning weapons or defending themselves against acts of aggression from Arab extremists. Those who attempted to do so were imprisoned.[lxx]

In defiance of their own government's obligation to protect Jewish inhabitants of the region, some British officers went so far as to encourage the Palestinian Arabs to use terrorism against the Jews in hopes the violence would cause Britain to abandon the idea of a Jewish state.[lxxi]

> These officers took significant measures to make life difficult for the Jewish people, who were prohibited from owning weapons or defending themselves against acts of aggression from Arab extremists.

THE PEEL COMMISSION

In 1936, the British government appointed a commission of inquiry led by William Robert Wellesley Peel in response to the Arab Revolt against the British Mandate and the ongoing violence directed at Jews by Arabs. The Palestine Royal Commission, informally known as the Peel Commission, was assigned to assess the causes of the Arab riots and evaluate the performance of the British Mandate government.

The Commission published a report on July 7, 1937, stating that the League of Nations Mandate had become unworkable because the Jewish and Arab objectives in Palestine were incompatible. Consequently, the report recommended partition.

The proposal divided Palestine into three zones: one for an Arab state, one for a Jewish state, and a neutral territory that would include the holy sites. Although the British government initially accepted these proposals, by 1938, it became clear that such a partition would not be practical, leading to the rejection of the commission's report.

THE BRITISH WHITE PAPER OF 1939

As Europe prepared for war and the Arab Revolt in Palestine intensified, Great Britain reconsidered the commitments it had made to Jewish Zionists two decades earlier. Their updated policy was outlined in the White Paper released in May 1939.

The White Paper policy stated that Palestine would not be established as a Jewish or Arab state but rather as an independent state within 10 years. Jewish immigration to Palestine was limited to 75,000 people during the first five years, depending on the country's "economic absorptive capacity," and would thereafter rely on "Arab consent." Additionally, strict restrictions were imposed on land acquisition by Jews.

The Jewish Agency for Palestine condemned the White Paper, stating that the British were denying the Jewish people their rights during what they described as the "darkest hour of Jewish history." This policy effectively closed the door to thousands of Jews who were desperately trying to escape Nazi persecution.

In another effort to appease Arab interests, the White Paper effectively denied European Jews the opportunity for refuge, leaving them exposed to the horrors of the Holocaust. This policy was viewed as a betrayal of the Balfour Declaration and represented a major setback for the Zionist movement in its pursuit of a Jewish homeland.

> **The White Paper effectively denied European Jews the opportunity for refuge, leaving them exposed to the horrors of the Holocaust.**

CHAPTER 26

Israel's Right to Exist

Initially, the British government established a partition of the land designated for a Jewish national home through the Mandate for Palestine. This partition allocated 77% of the land to an Arab state known as Transjordan, while 23% was designated for the Jewish people.

However, following the Arab riots of the 1920s and 1930s, Britain proposed another partition in 1937. This new plan allocated 80% of the land to an Arab state and 20% to a Jewish state. Palestinian Arab leaders, however, rejected this partition, and neither of the proposed states came into existence.[lxxii]

Frustrated by Arab rejectionism and in light of the atrocities committed against the Jews during the Holocaust, Britain transferred the responsibility for determining the future of Palestine to the newly established United Nations. On November 29, 1947, the United

Nations voted in favor of Resolution 181 and adopted a partition plan for Palestine that divided the land west of the Jordan River into two states roughly equal in size but noticeably unequal in value.

The fragmented pieces of land allocated for the Jewish people primarily consisted of barren desert lacking defensible borders and did not include Jerusalem, which was designated as an international zone. Even so, Jewish leaders, eager to re-establish a national home and provide refuge for the displaced Jews who had survived the Holocaust, accepted the plan.

Arab leaders publicly announced their intention to reject any proposal that included the establishment of a Jewish state. They acted on this promise by launching large-scale attacks on Jewish communities. Tragically, hundreds of Jews were killed in pogroms and other acts of terror between November 29, 1947, and the day Israel officially declared its independence on May 14, 1948.

Israel's existence as a Jewish state in the midst of what was once an Islamic empire was unacceptable to Arab leaders. Like Husseini, they effectively exploited anti-Jewish sentiments fueled by fabricated fears regarding their Muslim holy sites in Jerusalem. These false accusations stirred up a wave of antisemitism among their people.

The Palestinian Arabs gained the backing of five Arab armies to launch a war of annihilation against the Jewish state. Calls for war were framed in terms of jihad or "holy war." As soon as the British left Israel, the Arab armies attacked. Egypt, Syria, Transjordan, Lebanon, and Iraq invaded Israel while the international community stood back and silently watched.[lxxiii]

In a miraculous display of resilience and courage, Israel emerged victorious. However, they paid a heavy price, losing 1% of their total population (over 6,000 Israelis at the time) in defense of their God-given nation.

To avoid further disgrace and loss of territory, the Arab states signed an armistice agreement with Israel in 1949. However, the Arabs' insatiable objective of destroying Israel remained. From its founding until present day, Israel's enemies have made numerous attempts to wipe the Jewish nation off the map.

Thousands of Israelis have lost their lives in defense of their beloved homeland since its rebirth, culminating with the massacre of over 1,200 innocent Jews and the kidnapping and torture of over 250 hostages on October 7, 2023.

CHAPTER 27

The Mizrahi Jews

In retaliation for their crushing defeat, Muslim countries in the Middle East and North Africa initiated the harsh persecution of their native Jewish population, known as the Mizrahi Jews. This persecution was unexpected since the Jewish people had lived in many of these regions for over 2,500 years.[lxxiv]

By 1948, nearly one million Mizrahi Jews resided in Algeria, Egypt, Iran, Iraq, Libya, Lebanon, Morocco, Syria, Tunisia, Turkey, and Yemen. They had thriving businesses, well-established schools, and religious centers and spoke Arabic like their Muslim neighbors.

Yet after Israel was established as a nation, they were treated as the enemy. During the next few decades, nearly 850,000 Mizrahi Jews were forcibly

> Yet after Israel was established as a nation, they were treated as the enemy.

removed from their homes, had their wealth and possessions confiscated, and were expelled from the Middle Eastern countries they had inhabited for centuries.

Some immigrated to America, some to Europe, but many to Israel. The reborn Jewish state welcomed the Mizrahi refugees, gave them citizenship, and provided as much government assistance as possible to establish new lives, helping them to thrive in their Biblical homeland. Today, over half of Israel's population has descended from Mizrahi Jewish refugees.

> **The reborn Jewish state welcomed the Mizrahi refugees, gave them citizenship, and provided as much government assistance as possible to establish new lives, helping them to thrive in their Biblical homeland.**

CHAPTER 28

The Evolution of Antisemitic Terrorism and Propaganda

During the British Mandate period, Arab extremists aiming to destroy Israel discovered the devastating impact of terrorism. Deadly violence was not only an effective political weapon against the Jewish state, weakening it from within, but it also generated external pressure on the nation from the international community. The widespread dissemination of inflammatory misinformation within liberal media outlets fueled the runaway propaganda machine.

A typical example of the inversion of the truth and reality scheme is the accusation that the Jewish people,

> **A typical example of the inversion of the truth and reality scheme is the accusation that the Jewish people, who were victims of the Nazis, have now become the new Nazis — the aggressors and oppressors of the Palestinian Arabs.**

who were victims of the Nazis, have now become the new Nazis — the aggressors and oppressors of the Palestinian Arabs. This subversive method of "disinformation warfare" is also described as a "reversal of moral responsibility" or a form of "twisted logic" and an "inversion of reality."

Inversion of reality is a unique form of warfare that is a product of Nazi psychological manipulation. It is tyrannical in its methods, especially in using paranoid lies and in the extreme outcome it promotes. It constitutes the basic principle of contemporary anti-Israeli propaganda, still denying all of Israel's claims to the land and leaving no room for any resolution to the conflict.

For nearly half a century, Israel's adversaries have repeated these and other lies and character assassinations without being challenged or questioned. As a result, the denigration of the Jewish people and nation has gradually gained credibility.

The incessant goal of eradicating Israel in the 20th century fueled the rise of several Islamic extremist factions. Fundamental to each of these terrorist groups is an antisemitic interpretation of Islamic theology that leaves no room for the recognition of the State of Israel, the Jewish people, and, consequently, the possibility for lasting peace.[lxxv]

CHAPTER 29

The Muslim Brotherhood

The Muslim Brotherhood was among the earliest extremist groups to emerge in the region. The Brotherhood is a Sunni Islamist organization founded in 1928 in Egypt by Islamic scholar Hassan al-Banna. Its primary goal was to restore Islamic Sharia law (Islamic religious law) and re-establish an Islamic Sunni Caliphate (Islamic State) in the Middle East.

Soon after its inception, the Brotherhood adopted violent antisemitism as part of its ideology, repeatedly threatening and attacking Jews in the region. They admired Hitler's plan to eliminate the Jews widely distributing Arabic translations of Hitler's *Mein Kampf* and *The Protocols of the Elders of Zion*.[lxxvi]

The radical Islamic scholar and teacher Sayyid Qutb joined the Muslim Brotherhood in 1950. Through the Muslim Brotherhood, Qutb sought to eradicate Western influence from Egyptian society using the application of Sharia (Islamic Law). He shared the Brotherhood's hatred for the Jews, describing them as "nefarious agents of Satan" who planned to destroy Islam and corrupt society's morals.

Qutb relied on *The Protocols of the Elders of Zion* to "prove" his accusations against the Jews, leaving no room for the possibility that there could be such a thing as "a good Jew." His solution for the Jewish "threat" was the same as all other antisemites since Haman — total extermination.[lxxvii]

The Muslim Brotherhood laid the ideological foundations for the rise of both Sunni and Shia Islamist extremist groups. The Brotherhood declared that it is incumbent on all Muslims to wage jihad (holy war) worldwide to "liberate" non-Muslim lands from the infidels.[lxxviii] This rise of violent jihad as the supreme responsibility of all Muslims also encouraged the willingness to be a "martyr" and spawned the diabolic phenomenon of suicide attacks.

By the 1960s, the Muslim Brotherhood had exported its antisemitic ideology and fanatic devotion to jihad across the globe. The radical extremist theology and political goals of these groups evolved rapidly from the desire to win back lands that had once been under Islamic rule to a desire to conquer and dominate the entire world under Sharia law. These remain their goals to this day.

Although weakened by internal strife, nearly every major radical Islamist terrorist group of the last 50 years can trace its ideological roots back to the Muslim Brotherhood and the teachings of Sayyid Qutb. In the West, the Brotherhood founded "non-violent" Islamic institutions that preached the same hateful radical ideology while funneling money from its so-called charities to terrorist organizations around the globe.[lxxix]

The Brotherhood has historical ties to Hamas, as both groups operated alongside each other in Egypt until 2017. The Egyptian government is concerned about the possibility of the Muslim Brotherhood's resurgence in the country, causing instability in their nation, especially in light of the ongoing conflict in the Gaza Strip.

Qatar substantially underwrites both Hamas and the Brotherhood and allows their leaders to reside in Doha, Qatar's capital. Despite ongoing efforts to dismantle the Muslim Brotherhood, sleeper cells await opportunities to carry out attacks around the globe.

Egyptian intelligence is especially worried about the potential for Hamas operatives from Gaza to enter Egyptian territory after the war in Gaza. There is a concern that these individuals could collaborate with affiliates of the Muslim Brotherhood and ISIS in North Sinai, launching coordinated terrorist attacks against the Egyptian regime.[lxxx]

CHAPTER 30

The Palestinian Liberation Organization

The Palestinian Liberation Organization, or PLO, was founded in 1964 during the first Arab summit in Cairo, where leaders of 13 Arab nations pledged to take a more active role in the "liberation of Palestine." Since then, it has declared itself the representative of the Palestinian people and their nationalist aspirations. The PLO's national charter declared its intent to overthrow the State of Israel, which it called an "illegal colonial entity."[lxxxi]

The PLO primarily functions as an umbrella organization for six Palestinian groups, with Yasser Arafat's Fatah being the most prominent. In 1969, Arafat was elected Chairman of the PLO, establishing Fatah as its dominant party. Fatah eventually led to the formation of the Palestinian Authority in 1994.

The Palestinian leadership has considered the entire State of Israel an illegitimate presence ever since 1948, even though a Jewish remnant has remained in the land for nearly 4,000 years. The PLO's charter declared that the entire region designated as the British Mandate for Palestine in 1920, which includes all of modern Israel and Jordan, rightfully belongs to the Palestinian Arabs. It stated that only Jews who were living in the land before 1917 had the right to remain.

The charter also stated that every present and future child descending from a Palestinian Arab living in the land before 1947 is considered a Palestinian refugee, regardless of their citizenship status in any other country. Finally, the PLO's charter stated that violence was the only way to liberate Palestine from the Zionist presence.[lxxxii]

During the 1960s and 1970s, the PLO was based in Jordan and Lebanon. However, it launched deadly attacks against Israel and Jews worldwide, resulting in the loss of life for thousands of Israelis.

BLACK SEPTEMBER

An affiliate of the PLO, known as Black September, gained notoriety in the early 1970s for executing several significant terror attacks against the Jewish people.

The radical group was responsible for the massacre of 11 members of Israel's Olympic team at the 1972 Summer Games in Munich and the hijacking of a Belgian airliner in Vienna bound for Tel Aviv. Ninety passengers were taken hostage while the radicals demanded the release of 315 Palestinian terrorists from Israeli prisons. Israel's defense teams rescued all but one hostage.[lxxxiii]

In December 1974, Black September was disbanded by Fatah, likely in response to pressure from the Israeli Mossad. However, most of its members were reassigned to other Palestinian groups.

THE POPULAR FRONT FOR THE LIBERATION OF PALESTINE

In 1976, two members of the PLO faction and two German terrorist sympathizers hijacked a flight from Paris and forced the plane to land at Entebbe Airport in Uganda.[lxxxiv]

After landing, the terrorists freed the non-Jewish passengers and took 103 Jewish passengers hostage. For a week, Israel's government negotiated with the terrorists while the IDF organized a daring rescue mission.

Once Operation Entebbe began, the hostages were rescued within an hour. Israel lost three people that day — two hostages and the leader of the operation, Yoni Netanyahu. Yoni's brother Benjamin would become the Prime Minister of Israel and has served in that capacity longer than anyone in Israel's history.

In 1978, a raid by the PLO from Lebanon resulted in the hijacking of an Israeli bus filled with civilians, leading to the deaths of 34 hostages. In response, the IDF crossed the Lebanese border to drive the terrorists further north. This conflict lasted four years, during which PLO terrorists hiding in Lebanon continued to carry out hundreds of attacks on Israelis.[lxxxv]

Finally, after a Palestinian attempt to assassinate Israel's ambassador to Great Britain, Israel could no longer tolerate the buildup of a massive PLO army in Lebanon. On June 6, 1982, the IDF launched a full-scale war of self-defense to root out Yasser Arafat and his terrorists from southern Lebanon. The First Lebanon War, known as Operation Peace for Galilee, lasted until May 31, 1985, and cost 1,216 Israeli soldiers their lives.[lxxxvi]

YASSER ARAFAT

Arafat was a terrorist, a cold-blooded killer who had more Jewish blood on his hands than any man in the 20th century other than Adolf Hitler. As the leader of the PLO, Arafat aimed to harness the passion for "revolution" and "armed struggle" throughout the region. He was more effective in his efforts when he and his movement asserted that they were engaged in a struggle against Israel in the West Bank and Gaza Strip.

Yasser Arafat disguised himself as a "diplomat" representing the Palestinian people, deceiving the world while simultaneously authorizing acts of terrorism through groups like Black September. In fact, Arafat perfected the global propaganda tactic against the Jewish nation that had been effective in years past.

By 1974, he was addressing the United Nations, and on November 10, 1975, the UN General Assembly passed Resolution 3379, which

> **The UN General Assembly passed Resolution 3379, which determined that "Zionism is a form of racism and racial discrimination."**

determined that "Zionism is a form of racism and racial discrimination."

Arafat appeared to be gaining ground, leading to the Israeli invasions of 1978 and 1982. Arafat left Beirut for Tunisia in 1982. He later went back to Gaza in 1994 for what he hoped would be a triumphant return to a future Palestinian state.

Yasser Arafat returned to the Palestinian territories in the same year that South Africa held its first full and free elections, marking the end of apartheid. At that time, democracy was spreading worldwide. The Berlin Wall had fallen, and conflicts were concluding across the globe. The United States was a global leader overseeing this new world order.

When Israel withdrew from Lebanon in May 2000, Arafat had the opportunity to establish a state. However, he chose to pursue war instead. He concluded that Israel's withdrawal indicated that if the Jewish nation were pressured further through violence, it would ultimately give up.

In September 2000, Arafat believed that Ariel Sharon's visit to the Temple Mount could trigger a new uprising. As planned, clashes erupted in Gaza and quickly spread, marking the beginning of the Second Intifada. However, this intifada was different from the first one, (1987-1993) which facilitated Arafat's return to Gaza and contributed to the establishment of the Palestinian Authority (PA).

Instead, the Second Intifada was characterized by intense violence, including bus bombings, stabbings, and other widespread acts of terror, resulting in substantial loss of life within Israeli communities.

After his death in 2004, Yasser Arafat left a chaotic and corrupt Palestinian Authority in the hands of Mahmoud Abbas. Abbas allowed Hamas to win the Palestinian elections and subsequently permitted Hamas to expel Fatah from Gaza.

Although Abbas relied on the US-trained PA Security Forces to maintain his grip on power, his regime slowly became insignificant. The United Nations and various non-governmental organizations (NGOs) collaborated with Hamas in Gaza, and by 2012, Hamas leaders were in Doha, Qatar, being prepared for greater roles.

Several wars later, Hamas was prepared to launch the October 7 massacre, the goal of which was to end the concept of two states forever and plunge Israel into endless wars so that Hamas could eventually take over the West Bank.[lxxxvii]

THE LONE WOLF

The incitement to violence against Jews and extreme antisemitic rhetoric coming from the PLO, Hamas, Hezbollah, and other radical Islamic groups inspired a new breed of terrorism inside Israel, especially in Judea, and Samaria. Whereas previous terror attacks are usually planned and carried out by organized cells, "lone wolf" attacks are executed by individuals without any guidance, operational involvement, or organizational support of terrorist organizations.

Even though these terrorists act independently, they are very much inspired by groups like ISIS and Al-Qaeda. The terror organizations create support for "lone wolf" attacks through propaganda disseminated on-line, encouraging their supporters worldwide to attack Jews within their local communities. In the "Knife Intifada" of 2015-2016, Lone Wolf terrorists murdered 60 innocent Israelis.[lxxxviii]

In early 2018, the United States passed a law restricting American foreign aid to the Palestinian Authority until it ends this "Pay to Slay" program.

PAY TO SLAY

The PLO encourages attacks against Israelis by providing pensions and salaries to the terrorists and their families. In early 2018, the United States passed a law restricting American foreign aid to the Palestinian Authority until it ends this "Pay to Slay" program. However, in defiance, the PA announced that it was increasing the budget for this terrorist incentive from $347 million to $403 million.[lxxxix]

In February 2025, Palestinian Authority President Mahmoud Abbas rebutted reports that he had ended the PA's "martyr payments" at the 12th session of Fatah's Revolutionary Council. Abbas vowed that the PA would continue paying terrorists who kill Israelis and their families "even if we have only one cent left" and declared that "those who carry out terror attacks against Israelis are more precious than all of us combined."[xc]

CHAPTER 31

Hezbollah

In 1979, the radical Shia Muslim leader Ayatollah Khomeini overthrew the secular government of Iran and instituted the Islamic Revolution. Inspired by the writings of Sayyid Qutb and the ideology of the Muslim Brotherhood, Khomeini reinterpreted Shia theology and transformed the historically peaceful religious minority sect into one committed to violent jihad.[xci]

As Qutb had done for extremist Sunni Muslims, Khomeini combined historical antisemitism and stories of ancient Jewish foes with the myths of European antisemitism, portraying Jews as satanic, bloodthirsty creatures bent on world domination and societal corruption.[xcii]

During the 1980s, Iran's radical government focused heavily on global jihad against Israel, Jews, and their allies. Seizing the opportunity to export his Islamic Revolution's ideology of holy war against the Jews, Ayatollah

Khomeini dispatched the Iranian Revolutionary Guard Corps (IRGC) to southern Lebanon.

There, they established and trained a new terrorist group known as Hezbollah, Arabic for "Party of God." As Israel worked to remove the PLO from Lebanon in 1982, Hezbollah was created with the explicit mission to destroy Israel as a proxy of the Iranian government.[xciii]

After Israel withdrew from Lebanon, Hezbollah remained and grew stronger until it became a dominant political and military force in the country, effectively placing the Lebanese government under the thumb of Iran.[xciv]

In collaboration with Iran, Hezbollah has become one of the deadliest terror organizations in the world, spreading its antisemitic terror across the globe. Its motivation is its twisted theology that blames every social and political problem on the Jews.

During the 1990s, Hezbollah sent its operatives to Argentina, where they bombed the Israeli Embassy in Buenos Aires. Two years later, they bombed a Jewish community center in the same city. In 2012, Hezbollah bombed an Israeli tour bus in Bulgaria.[xcv]

Hassan Nasrallah, a Lebanese cleric who served as Hezbollah's Secretary-General from 1992 until his assassination in 2024, stated that he viewed all Jews around the world as targets for extermination. In an excerpt reported by Lebanon's *The Daily Star*, Nasrallah was quoted as saying, "If they [Jews] all gather in Israel, it will save us the trouble of going after them worldwide."

Iran and Hezbollah made no secret of their desire to complete Hitler's mission of eradicating the Jewish people from the face of the earth. It seems ironic that the Iranian regime both denies and glorifies the history of the Holocaust, all the while seeking to perpetrate a new one.[xcvi]

> **Iran and Hezbollah made no secret of their desire to complete Hitler's mission of eradicating the Jewish people from the face of the earth.**

Hezbollah entered the war on October 8, 2023, one day after Hamas' ground attack on southern Israel. Their objective was to sufficiently attack Israel's northern border, forcing them to accept a ceasefire with Hamas. The militant group began launching almost daily drone, missile, and rocket attacks targeting towns and military sites

THE MIDDLE EAST CONFLICT

in northern Israel. These strikes caused nearly 250,000 Israeli citizens to evacuate, leaving many of them displaced for over a year.

In the summer of 2024, Israel launched major military operations in Lebanon to deter Hezbollah from continuing its barrage of missiles. The campaign began with airstrikes targeting key leaders, including Hassan Nasrallah. It also involved the detonation of thousands of pagers and handheld radios belonging to Hezbollah members across Lebanon.

Israel's actions disrupted Hezbollah's operations and temporarily weakened the group. Capitalizing on this disruption, the IDF launched ground operations against the disorganized Hezbollah forces in southern Lebanon. They cleared the border towns and seized key terrain, including ridgelines that Hezbollah used for launching attacks into northern Israel.

> Israel's actions disrupted Hezbollah's operations and temporarily weakened the group.

On November 26, 2023, Israel and Hezbollah reached a ceasefire agreement that halted Hezbollah's assaults on Israel and required the group to disarm in southern Lebanon. The victory allowed Israel to safely return the majority of its displaced citizens to their homes in northern Israel. The ceasefire also guaranteed Israel's right to self-defense against any potential future threats from Hezbollah.[xcvii]

Hezbollah's defeat significantly diminished its strength. However, Iran's proxy will likely begin to rebuild its forces and attempt to re-establish its dominance in Lebanon.

The victory allowed Israel to safely return the majority of its displaced citizens to their homes in northern Israel.

CHAPTER 32

Al-Qaeda

The revival of Islamic fundamentalism and the subsequent calls for holy war against Jews and other so-called enemies of Islam led to Iran's Islamic Revolution, the emergence of Hezbollah, and the formation of Al-Qaeda (AQ). The organization operated out of Sudan and later re-established its headquarters in Afghanistan around the mid-90s under the sponsorship of the Taliban militia.

Al-Qaeda, founded by Osama bin Laden, became one of the world's most notorious terrorist organizations after carrying out the September 11, 2001, attacks on the United States. Bin Laden was also heavily influenced by the antisemitic writings of Sayyid Qutb, adopting the theology of jihad as a core component of his beliefs.[xcviii]

Al-Qaeda began as a logistical network to support Muslims fighting against the Soviet Union during the Afghan War. When the Soviets withdrew from

Afghanistan in 1989, the organization continued to oppose what its leaders considered corrupt Islamic regimes and foreign presence, such as the U.S., in Islamic lands.

Hamas and Al-Qaeda have vastly different ideological views — although both are ruthless. After July 2007, Hamas began cracking down on affiliates that were ideologically allied with Al-Qaeda in Gaza. Guns were turned against fellow Muslims, and there were calls for insurrection by the "honest" mujahideen (those who struggle) against the Hamas leadership.

In Al-Qaeda's version of events, "doctrinal deviation had led to methodological deviation." It was Hamas that had sinned and rejected God; now, Hamas would pay with open war.[xcix]

Interestingly, Al-Qaeda and Osama bin Laden's successors have formed an unexpected partnership with the Republic of Iran despite their differing Islamic beliefs. What unites them is a shared hatred for Israel and the United States, Israel's primary ally.

Since the October 7 attack, the senior leadership of Al-Qaeda has sought to regain relevance by provoking international outrage over Israel's military response. As a result, it has aligned itself more closely with Hamas, a group it has historically criticized. Additionally, reports suggest that Al-Qaeda has established a new affiliate in Gaza to capitalize on the current situation.[c]

CHAPTER 33

ISIS

Al-Qaeda produced a radical and barbaric splinter group now known as the Islamic State in Iraq and Syria (ISIS).[ci]

In 2014, President Obama infamously dismissed ISIS as the "JV team." Still, the world soon learned how wrong his assumption was and witnessed a surge in mass-casualty terrorism at the hands of ISIS fanatics.

ISIS's goal of establishing an Islamic caliphate in the Middle East was not achieved due to losses in Syria and Iraq, partly aided by President Trump's military efforts to eliminate ISIS in Syria. However, ISIS has been extraordinarily successful at exporting its antisemitic and anti-Western theology over the internet to a new generation of homegrown terrorists across the globe. ISIS has redirected its focus from establishing a caliphate to the war with Israel. The brutal ideology of ISIS was evident in the deplorable actions of Hamas during the massacre on October 7, 2023.

CHAPTER 34

Hamas

Hamas, an Arabic acronym for the Islamic Resistance Movement, was created by the Muslim Brotherhood in the 1980s. Hamas was originally a social welfare organization for the benefit of Palestinians in Gaza.[cii]

However, this radical group quickly transformed into a terrorist group dedicated to attacking Israel and brutally enforcing strict Islamic law on the Palestinians under its influence.

Hamas rose to power due to the frustration of certain Palestinian extremists with Yasser Arafat's political engagement with Israel and

> **This radical group quickly transformed into a terrorist group dedicated to attacking Israel and brutally enforcing strict Islamic law on the Palestinians under its influence.**

his promises to limit the PLO and Fatah party's support for terrorism. In reality, Arafat was merely posturing to gain sympathy from the United Nations. He never renounced terrorism, but by giving lip service to the idea of compromise with Israel, he angered Islamist radicals. Consequently, Hamas recruited a more extreme group of terrorists than the PLO and committed itself to the total destruction of Israel.[ciii]

In 2006, Israel unilaterally withdrew from the Gaza Strip to build goodwill with the Palestinians and reduce the IDF's responsibilities in the area. However, Hamas capitalized on the power vacuum created by this withdrawal and quickly won the elections in 2007.

The political defeat led to the Fatah-led Palestinian Authority government being expelled from Gaza. The immediate results of the election were catastrophic as Hamas began relentless missile attacks on Israel and executed Palestinians who were suspected of sympathizing or collaborating with its political opponents or Israel.[civ]

Hamas' charter, like that of Hezbollah, specifically dedicates itself to the total annihilation of the Jewish state. Like Hezbollah, Hamas intentionally targets Israeli civilians and uses its own

> **Hamas' charter, like that of Hezbollah, specifically dedicates itself to the total annihilation of the Jewish state.**

civilian population as human shields. Case in point, during the 2024 Swords of Iron Gaza War, IDF forces found stockpiles of munitions and rockets in school playgrounds, within Al-Shifa Hospital, UNRWA schools, and civilian neighborhoods.

One of the worst crimes against humanity perpetrated by these two terrorist organizations is their practice of deliberately hiding their weapons in civilian areas. This attempt to force Israel to kill innocent men, women, and children to defend itself from the terrorists is a calculated propaganda maneuver.[cv]

The purpose of this malicious strategy is clear: its goal is to incite global hatred against Israel, pushing the country to either commit national suicide by surrendering or face severe international political and economic repercussions for its acts of self-defense. This vile plan has been highly effective in assisting Israel's adversaries in depicting the Jewish nation as a ruthless oppressor. When in reality, it is Hamas and Hezbollah who are accountable for war crimes under international law.

Since 2006, Hamas has launched tens of thousands of rockets into Israel, instigated numerous terrorist plots, kidnapped Israeli soldiers, and attempted to infiltrate Jewish neighborhoods by tunneling under the border with Gaza. However, the most vicious and deadly of these attacks was the massacre of October 7, 2023.

Remember this truth — Hamas has no interest in a Palestinian state alongside Israel, regardless of whatever concessions Israel is willing to make.

Hamas' fight for control of the Palestinians in Judea and Samaria, and its growing popularity there, threatens Fatah and undermines any future agreement within these terrorist factions.

Palestinian Authority President Mahmoud Abbas' Fatah party vowed not to "allow Hamas, which sacrificed the interests of the Palestinian people for Iran and caused destruction in the Gaza Strip, to replicate its actions in the West Bank."[cvi]

WHAT WENT WRONG

In late February of 2025, investigations into failures by Israel's Military Intelligence Directorate revealed that the IDF received plans detailing a possible ground attack in 2022 but considered it unlikely. They viewed Yahya Sinwar as a realist who did not want to engage in another confrontation with Israel.

The IDF has now determined that Hamas had decided in April 2022 to launch a large ground invasion against Israel. By September 2022, the terror group was 85% ready, and in May, they set the date to October 7, 2023.

Hamas' leaders, who had lain low for two years after a weeks-long fight with Israel in 2021, took advantage of Israel that October Saturday and burst forth over the border on the Jewish holiday of Simchat Torah, knowing fewer troops were along the border than usual.

The investigations revealed three significant failures in Israeli intelligence that overlooked a possible Hamas attack on southern Israel.

1. The Intelligence Directorate failed to comprehend Hamas' capability, especially following the 2021 Gaza War, to include the incorrect assessments of Hamas' strategy, aspirations, plans, and military capabilities.

2. The Intelligence Directorate's failure to consider Hamas' surprise attack and the events leading up to it.

3. The Intelligence Directorate's limited use of surveillance to obtain critical information on Hamas.

The main conclusion of the investigation is that Israel cannot permit threats to escalate along its borders, as it did with Hamas and Hezbollah. The report recommends that Israel create an intelligence unit that evaluates warning signals, significantly expanding the military and enhancing border defenses.[cvii]

CHAPTER 35

The Houthis

The Houthis emerged as a bloodthirsty player in the Israel-Hamas war. Backed by Iran, the Houthis are an extremist Shia-Islamist movement and terrorist army. This organization controls approximately one-third of Yemen's territory and more than two-thirds of the country's population, with the intent to dominate all of Yemen.

With support from Iran, the Houthis pose a major challenge in the Middle East. Like their benefactor, their ideology aims to reshape the region through destruction and warfare. Their aggressive actions, such as launching missiles toward Israel and other countries and attacking and hijacking commercial sea vessels, underscore the group's intent to extend its influence beyond Yemen's borders.

Since late 2023, Houthi militants have launched ballistic missiles and suicide drones into Israel, reaching as far as downtown Tel Aviv. The group has also violated international maritime law by hijacking commercial vessels in the Red Sea, posing a direct threat to international shipping and the global economy. Most of these threats have been intercepted by Israel's multi-layered air defense system or by U.S. warships.

In response to ongoing tensions, Israel has conducted several airstrikes targeting Houthi-controlled infrastructure in Yemen. These strikes have focused on key locations, including ports, oil facilities, and the airport in the capital city of Sanaa.

Additionally, the United States has also taken military action against the Houthis. In December 2024, U.S. forces carried out precision strikes in Yemen following attacks on American warships and commercial vessels in the Red Sea. Israeli air defenses successfully intercepted ballistic missiles launched at Israel by the Houthis in May 2025. In both instances, sirens sounded across central Israel, including Tel Aviv, sending nearly a million residents scrambling for bomb shelters. The Houthis claimed they targeted Ben Gurion Airport, vowing to continue the strikes until Israel's "siege is lifted" on Gaza. Just days after taking office, President Donald Trump re-designated the Houthi terror group as a Foreign Terrorist Organization.

CHAPTER 36

Iran

Clearly, the unholy war against the Jews over the last century and the emphasis on violent jihad in the last 40 years are far from over. Although radical Islamic terror groups compete with each other, they are united in their intense hatred of Israel and the Jewish people.

The spirit of Hitler lives on in their theology, their political discourse, their brainwashing youth programs, and their culture of death worship. This deep obsession with Jew hatred inspires their followers to value death more than life and produce suffering for millions of innocent people — both Arab and Jewish.

> **The spirit of Hitler lives on in their theology, their political discourse, their youth brainwashing programs, and their culture of death worship.**

THE IRAN DEAL

Iran and its proxies were on the verge of bankruptcy as a result of world economic sanctions, yet, astonishingly, in July of 2015, the United Nations Security Council adopted the "Iran Deal," which released over one billion dollars into Iran's coffers. As bad as this was, the situation got worse.

In the fall of 2016, President Obama authorized spending an additional 1.7 billion dollars under the guise of paying back a deposit ($400 million) plus interest ($1.3 billion) that we supposedly "owed" due to a failed arms deal with the Shah of Iran in 1979. To add insult to injury, this "payback" was not wired bank to bank but sent to Iran using U.S. military cargo planes, carrying various unmarked world currencies and denominations.

It is reasonable to assume that this covert transfer of funds, which represented a betrayal of the Jewish state, was intended for illegal transactions. In essence, our tax dollars financed Iran's significant buildup of missiles in Lebanon, which were used against Israel, America's only reliable ally in the Middle East.

Iran's tentacles are far-reaching, and their goal is to eradicate Israel and wipe out the Western world's way of life — no matter the cost. Iran invests billions of dollars in funding its military, Hezbollah, Hamas, and the rest of its terrorist networks. Its objective is the destabilization of the entire Middle East.

Looming above it is the dark shadow of Iran's ambition for a nuclear holocaust that threatens to spark a third world war. On April 30, 2018, Israeli Prime Minister Benjamin Netanyahu publicly revealed the existence of Iran's secret nuclear weapons program on international television. This disclosure confirmed our long-held belief that Iran's relentless pursuit of nuclear weapons through AMAD Project threatened global security.

The evidence of Iran's deceit and evil intent was publicly announced just two weeks before President Trump's deadline to fix or withdraw from the Iran Deal. These documents, which proved Iran lied to the International Atomic Energy Agency (IAEA), left no doubt that the Iran Deal was fatally flawed from the start.

> **These documents, which proved Iran lied to the International Atomic Energy Agency (IAEA), left no doubt that the Iran Deal was fatally flawed from the start.**

On May 8, 2018, President Trump announced that the United States would withdraw from the Iran Deal, also known as the Joint Comprehensive Plan of Action (JCPOA). He noted that the plan "didn't bring calm, it didn't bring peace, and it never will."

IRAN AND THE NUCLEAR BOMB

Even before the October 7, 2023 attacks, Iran had reached a critical point in nuclear weapons capability. It currently possesses the technologies and expertise necessary for the rapid development of nuclear weapons if a political decision is made to proceed.

In the final months of 2024, Iran significantly increased its capacity to enrich uranium to levels close to those suitable for weapons. Tehran announced plans to boost the production of enriched uranium to 60 % and use additional advanced centrifuges that operate more efficiently for enrichment.

Uranium is usually enriched to 90% for use as weapon fuel. However, enriching uranium from 60% to 90% is relatively simple. Iran's current stockpile of highly enriched uranium, along with its ability to increase enrichment quickly, would enable it to produce enough weapons-grade uranium for approximately five to six nuclear weapons within less than two weeks.

The increase in uranium production is alarming because it is happening at the Fordow Fuel Enrichment Plant, which is situated deep within a mountain. This location makes it challenging for Israel or the United States to target and destroy the facility if either country chooses to conduct a military strike to hinder Iran's nuclear program.

If Iran chooses to pursue the development of nuclear weapons, it has two potential pathways. The first option involves withdrawing from the Nuclear Non-Proliferation Treaty (NPT) and canceling its safeguards agreement. This action would eliminate international inspections, enabling Iran to utilize its declared nuclear facilities to produce sufficient uranium enriched to 90% for one nuclear weapon.

This decision would involve significant risks, as it would clearly confirm Iran's intention to develop a nuclear weapon. Such a move would also give the United States and Israel the chance to intervene and disrupt Iran's nuclear program.

By targeting declared nuclear sites, the U.S. and Israel could potentially prevent Iran from enriching enough material before it could be diverted to covert sites for weaponization. The alternative option is for Iran to secretly develop nuclear weapons.[cviii]

CHAPTER 37

American Leadership and Israel: 2016–Present

President Trump's first term (January 2017–January 2021) was marked by nothing short of historic actions related to the US-Israel relationship. Aside from President Harry Truman, who voted for Israel's statehood in 1948, President Trump did more for Israel and the Jewish people in his first term than any administration in history.

First and foremost, President Trump followed through on a decades-old U.S. law to move the U.S. Embassy from Tel Aviv to Jerusalem. What I said at the

> **President Trump followed through on a decades-old U.S. law to move the U.S. Embassy from Tel Aviv to Jerusalem.**

2018 benediction of the new U.S. Embassy in Jerusalem remains true today:

> "We thank you, O Lord, for President Donald Trump's courage in acknowledging to the world a truth that was established 3,000 years ago — that Jerusalem is and always shall be the eternal capital of the Jewish people. And because of that courage of our president, we gather here today to consecrate the ground upon which the United States Embassy will stand, reminding the dictators of the world that America and Israel are forever united."

But President Trump did not stop there; a year later, he issued a proclamation recognizing the strategically vital Golan Heights as sovereign Israeli land. By moving forward with the recognition, the Trump administration sent an important message to Israel's enemies: America stands with Israel now and forever to ensure that she has defensible borders.

Between Israel's War of Independence and the 1967 Six-Day War, Israeli civilians living below the Golan Heights faced constant attacks.

Between Israel's War of Independence and the 1967 Six-Day War, Israeli civilians living below the Golan Heights faced constant attacks. This was followed by the 1973 Yom Kippur War, in which the Egyptian and Syrian military forces launched a surprise attack against Israel. In both instances, Israel was fighting a clearly defensive war of survival. President Trump's historic proclamation ensured that Israel would never be in a position where it did not maintain the high ground on its northern border.

In December 2019, President Trump signed a groundbreaking executive order that adopted the International Holocaust Remembrance Alliance (IHRA) definition of antisemitism for the federal government and the Department of Education. We did not know at that time just how critical this executive order would be in a few short years when vicious antisemitism swept across college campuses throughout our country.

What President Trump did was particularly important in countering antisemitism because you cannot defeat what you will not define.

The Trump administration also took a hardline approach to Israel's enemies by pressuring international organizations and terror states like Iran through a series of maximum actions. He withheld U.S. funding from antisemitic outfits like UNRWA (The United Nations Relief and Works Agency), sending a strong message that the Palestinian policy of "pay to slay" would not be funded by American taxpayer dollars.

During his first term, President Trump successfully negotiated four peace agreements between Israel and several Arab-Muslim nations, collectively known as the Abraham Accords.

On August 13, 2020, Israel and the United Arab Emirates agreed to normalize their relations, marking the first peace agreement between an Arab country and Israel in over 25 years. Additionally, Saudi Arabia permitted commercial flights to Israel to utilize its airspace for the first time in over 70 years.

Under President Trump, Israel and Bahrain normalized their relations on September 11, 2020. Weeks later, Israel and Sudan agreed to normalize their relations on October 23, 2020, and Israel and Morocco agreed to full diplomatic relations on December 10, 2020.

President Trump facilitated economic normalization between Serbia and Kosovo, which included both nations agreeing to open embassies in Jerusalem. Additionally, the United States withdrew from the United

Nations Human Rights Council due to the organization's blatant anti-Israel bias.

The first few weeks of **President Trump's second term (January 2025–Present)** have been no less important. The administration has moved quickly to enact changes to U.S. policy as it relates to Israel, our shared enemies, and the fight against antisemitism by:

- Reversing holds on key weapons for the Israel Defense Forces that were in place by the Biden Administration.

- Doubling down on the 2019 executive order to combat antisemitism by issuing a new and more comprehensive executive order to further pressure college campuses to take action against the spread of antisemitism.

- Establishing a new Department of Justice task force to combat antisemitism.

- Returning to the policy of maximum pressure on the Islamic Republic of Iran.

- Withdrawing funding once again from the likes of UNRWA and the Palestinian Authority.

- Hosting Israel's Prime Minister Benjamin Netanyahu as the first foreign leader to visit the White House.

- Approving new transfers of roughly $12 billion worth of weapons and other military hardware to Israel.[cix]

Unfortunately, **the Biden Administration (January 2021–2024)** had a complicated relationship with Israel during its tenure. Although President Biden often expressed his support for Israel, describing himself as a Zionist — a statement that many pro-Israel advocates appreciate — his administration frequently appeared to take one step forward and two steps back in its dealings with Jerusalem.

The administration supported Israel as it faced a multi-front attack, both diplomatically and, most importantly, with a $14.3 billion arms package in the wake of the devastating October 7, 2023 attacks. However, it sought to micromanage Jerusalem's efforts to defeat Hamas and Hezbollah, often attempting to obstruct key military decisions undertaken by Israel.

Several of Israel's strategies have been validated, such as the IDF going into Rafah, where they found hostages and eliminated the October 7 mastermind, Yahya Sinwar.

Other elements of the Biden administration, particularly the State Department, even displayed hostility toward Israel. This included imposing sanctions on Israelis, threatening sanctions against certain IDF units, and withholding essential military equipment.

Additionally, the Biden administration did little to prevent the Iranian regime from advancing its nuclear weapons program. It also allowed international organizations to criticize Israel for defending itself against the brutal attacks from Iran's proxy armies.

In fact, from 2018 to 2023, the State Department issued temporary sanctions waivers that allowed Iraq to import electricity from Iran on the condition that all payments were kept in an escrow account in Baghdad, thereby denying Iran access to the revenue.

In the summer of 2024, the Biden administration changed that waiver to allow Iraq to transfer $10 billion to Iran and to deposit future payments into Iranian bank accounts in Oman. The new policy also permitted Iran to convert the money from Iraqi dinars to euros. Iran could then process euro-based transactions for imports and debt payments out of their accounts in Oman.

The Biden administration stated that the waiver was intended solely for Iraq to import electricity physically. However, this waiver released billions of dollars that Iran utilized for budget support. By allowing access to $10 billion or possibly more from Oman, it freed up an equal amount of funds that Tehran redirected to various uses, including terrorism, missile development, and nuclear capabilities.[cx]

In a U.S. House Hearing on government spending, the question was asked of a witness if he was aware that America was sending $40 million a week to the Taliban, a fundamentalist Islamic militia in Afghanistan.

The witness confirmed that fact and gave other instances where the U.S. funded terrorist groups like al-Shabaab in Somalia, the Hamzi network in Sudan, Hamas, Islamic Jihad, Hezbollah, Kata'ib Hezbollah, and Hay'at Tahrir al-Sham in Syria. The witness further confirmed that dozens more terror organizations had received indirect assistance from U.S. foreign aid.

The witness used Gaza as a case study. He testified that $2.1 billion in American taxpayers' money has been sent to Gaza since October 7, 2023. USAID funds were "intended" for emergency use and were meant to go to groups within the Gaza Strip that formerly had a relationship with USAID.

Under standard procedure, each organization had to be vetted against the designated terrorist list in the State Department and by other Treasury organizations. However, Biden's government officials granted waivers to the vetting process, thus abandoning the usual screening procedures.

As a result, 90% of the aid that was intended to go from the United States by way of its agents in Gaza ended up in Hamas-controlled areas. The witness went on to say, "Essentially, what the U.S. assistance to Gaza did was underwrite the ability for Hamas to survive until the cease-fire."

Furthermore, the hearings disclosed that a high-ranking administrator for USAID was intent on preventing Israel from being able to defend itself. Essentially, America, in many respects, was funding both sides of the Gazan conflict while preventing Israel to win the war against evil.

IT'S BIBLICAL

To be clear, the US-Israel relationship must remain bipartisan, and that is why the overwhelming majority of Republicans and Democrats in Congress have worked together across both the Trump and Biden administrations to support and strengthen the relationship.

This bond is not built on today's politics but on a Biblical mandate and strategic imperative that goes beyond any single American or Israeli leader — a relationship that Christians United for Israel works day in and day out to maintain and prosper.

CHAPTER 38

Antisemitism is Everyone's Problem

Antisemitism did not originate or end with Adolf Hitler. As detailed, the Jewish people have been persecuted since ancient times, and this unrivaled hatred against them lives on worldwide.

Jew hatred in America never advanced to the lethal level of Nazi-led Germany or the Hamas massacre of October 7, 2023, but it is widespread, nonetheless. Antisemitism has never fully disappeared from society; however, in the mid-40s, the horrors of the Holocaust significantly suppressed its public expression for a season.

As memories have faded and many survivors are no longer with us to share their stories, condemnation of the State of Israel and the Jewish people has grown. Antisemitism was, and in some cases still is, prevalent in social, religious, political, and educational circles and even within certain influential progressive movements.

In recent years, there has been a deeply concerning upsurge of antisemitism around the world, including in the United States. Some of the settings may have changed, but the hateful rhetoric remains the same — accusing the Jewish people of long-standing claims ranging from dual loyalty to using their evil power to control the world because they have a "disproportionate amount of political and economic power."

The manifestations of Jew hatred are becoming increasingly blatant as we witness an increase in violent antisemitic incidents throughout the world. We see it with the re-emergence of Replacement Theology in the church, within places of higher learning, through apartheid accusations, and the BDS movement (Boycott, Divestment, and Sanctions).

College campus students and tenured professors have become more comfortable with not only criticizing Israel but attacking Jewish students for simply being Jewish or because they support the ideals of the Jewish state. Furthermore, non-Jewish students are being spat upon for supporting their Jewish friends on campuses throughout America and the world.

Why have America's college campuses become a hotbed for antisemitism? Because the enemy knows that one hundred percent of the future belongs to the next generation. Here, hatred toward Israel is masked as a natural response to the baseless claims that the Jewish people are "the aggressors" of the "oppressed Palestinians" through an "apartheid regime" — one that discriminates on the grounds of race. This propaganda is ridiculous at best.

The rise of social media has led to a surge in antisemitic threats and a dramatic increase in militant Muslim extremism worldwide. The internet provides the "facelessness" that anti-Jewish extremists thrive on, sadly

> **The rise of social media has led to a surge in antisemitic threats and a dramatic increase in militant Muslim extremism worldwide. The internet provides the "facelessness" that anti-Jewish extremists thrive on, sadly allowing them the opportunity to influence millions with their false rhetoric.**

allowing them the opportunity to influence millions with their false rhetoric.

Before the Hamas massacre, a report in early 2018 showed a dramatic 57% increase in antisemitic incidents in America compared to 2016.[cxi] And the number of incidents on college campuses nearly doubled for two consecutive years. Moreover, antisemitic incidents were recorded in every state. In a report showing antisemitic incidents between 2014 and 2023 in the US, incidents increased from 912 to a staggering 8,873 — an 872% increase.[cxii]

Recently, *The Times of Israel* published a report by the Anti-Defamation League and Hillel International that 83 percent of Jewish American college students have experienced or witnessed antisemitism firsthand since October 7, 2023.

Recently, *The Times of Israel* published a report by the Anti-Defamation League and Hillel International that 83% of Jewish American college students have experienced or witnessed antisemitism firsthand since October 7, 2023.

The survey, which surveyed 1,030 Jewish and 1,140 non-Jewish students from 135 colleges and universities across the United States during the fall of 2024, revealed a troubling picture of Jewish campus life. Furthermore, the survey found that 66% of Jewish students and 60% of non-Jewish students believed that their universities were not able or willing to prevent antisemitic incidents.[cxiii] These numbers are deeply troubling.

Malcolm Hoenlein, a dear friend who serves as the Vice Chairman Emeritus of the Conference of Presidents of Major American Jewish Organizations, believes that for several years, it was accepted for Americans to say that they were *anti-Israel*. However, "Today, it is accepted to say I am *anti-Jewish*." This, Hoenlein believes, is partly due to the anti-Israel BDS, which provides a "cover for antisemitism."[cxiv]

No matter the reason, Jew hatred is once again spreading like a contagious virus. It is a cancer that is eating away the soul of America and the world. Some tag a sophisticated label on antisemitism. But it is still sin, and as sin, it damns the soul.

Antisemitism is not just a Jewish problem — it's the world's problem. I fully stand with Malcolm, who states:

"Combating antisemitism starts with the Jewish community, but it doesn't end with it. This is not our problem. It's society's problem. It's Christianity's problem. It's everybody's problem when there's hatred against Jews. We're the victims; we're not the cause of it. It's not because we did something wrong. It's because of who we are and our values."

Several years ago, I stated that our generation was headed for a perfect storm. But who would have thought that we would witness the Jew hatred displayed on America's streets and on college campuses after the horrors of October 7, 2023?

My friends, we are now standing at the center of that perfect storm, and we cannot stand idly by as so many Christians did during WWII. In order not to repeat the mistakes of the past, we must learn from this profound mandate made by Israeli Holocaust historian and scholar, Yehuda Bauer: *"Thou shalt not be a victim, thou shalt not be a perpetrator but, above all, thou shalt not be a bystander."*[cxv]

> *This time,* in world history, Christians must not stand idly by.
>
> *This time,* righteous people must take a stand.
>
> *This time,* we must circle the wagons and fight the battle against Jew hatred.
>
> *This time,* Christians and Jews must unite and win the war against antisemitism — together.

If a circle has to be drawn — then draw it around Christian and Jew — because we are one!

As Israel's enemies continue to conspire to eliminate her, I respond to their threats and actions with the words of Jeremiah:

*It is the L*ORD *who provides the sun to light the day and the moon and stars to light the night, and who stirs the sea into roaring waves. His name is the L*ORD *of Heaven's Armies, and this is what he says: "I am as likely to reject my people Israel as I am to abolish the laws of nature!"*
Jeremiah 31:35–36 (NLT)

CHAPTER 39

Israel is Eternal

The Bible declares, *"Your word, Lord, is eternal; it stands firm in the heavens"* (Psalm 119:89, NIV). First Kings speaks of the Lord's eternal love for Israel (10:9), and Genesis 17:7 establishes God's everlasting covenant with Abraham and his descendants.

If God's Word is eternal and true, and His love for Israel is everlasting, and His covenant with the Jewish people is forever, then Israel is also eternal.

Since Israel and the Jewish people are important to God, they should also be important to us. The Lord commands us to comfort His people and stand by them in their times of need (Isaiah 40:1). This comfort can take many forms. It may involve supporting humanitarian causes or taking action against the evil of antisemitism, which was the source of the tragic massacre on October 7.

We can also reassure our Jewish friends that they are not alone by speaking out against the pro-Hamas mobs protesting Israel's existence, which have contributed to the alarming rise in antisemitism. Additionally, we can challenge the anti-Jewish rhetoric that is being expressed on American campuses by those rioting in the streets and even with those supporting Hamas in Congress.

Since Abraham's time, the Jewish nation has been God's Chosen People. The God of Abraham, Isaac, and Jacob will protect His people, come what may, because His commitment to Israel is infinite and eternal. The question is, will you be among those the Lord uses to comfort, protect, and bless Israel and her people?

The message from Mordecai to Queen Esther remains relevant today: If we fail to support and protect God's Chosen People, their deliverance will come from another source (Esther 4:14). We have been appointed for this very moment in time.

I often hear Christians say that if they were alive during the Holocaust, they would have taken action to protect the Jewish people. However, what truly matters is that our Jewish brothers and sisters are facing attacks both at home and worldwide *today*. The question we must ask ourselves is: *What are we doing to help Israel and the Jewish people **right now**?*

As Israel fights for its survival and works to eliminate its enemies, we must take action during this critical hour. We cannot turn our backs! Israel has an important story to tell, and we must make sure it is heard.

Eighty years after the attempted extermination of the Jews by the Nazis, and even in the last two years since the Hamas Massacre of 2023, few people seem to remember the words, "NEVER AGAIN." This promise is a call to action against antisemitism and other forms of Jew hatred.

> **Our Jewish brothers and sisters are facing attacks both at home and worldwide *today*.**

> **We cannot turn our backs! Israel has an important story to tell, and we must make sure it is heard.**

CHAPTER 40

What Now?

You have already taken two crucial steps by reading and understanding the Biblical, historical, and present-day geopolitical context of the Jewish nation and its people. The first is equipping yourself with the Word of God, and the second is knowing the facts on the ground, ensuring that you are best positioned to bless and comfort Israel and the Jewish people.

As Christians, we are called to bless the Jewish people. God said to Abraham, *"I will bless those who bless you, and I will curse him who curses you; and in you all the families of the earth shall be blessed"* (Genesis 12:3). Hagee Ministries has stood in support of Israel for over 44 years. After the assault on the Jewish people on October 7, 2023, Hagee Ministries collaborated with

> **As Christians, we are called to bless the Jewish people.**

Christians United for Israel and its affiliated churches to provide comfort to the Jewish people by supporting humanitarian efforts within Israel, especially during times of war. You can advocate for the Jewish nation and her people by:

- Learning more about Christians United for Israel and becoming a partner with Hagee Ministries.

- Attending the CUFI National Summit in Washington, D.C., with thousands of other pro-Israel Christians and Jews, where you can learn from Middle East experts and visit your elected officials in support of Israel.

- Encouraging your church to participate with CUFI by hosting a Night to Honor Israel, a Pastor's Gathering, or a Why Israel? or Israel Is education event.

- Creating a small group in your community or home and study CUFI's *The Israel Course* and *CUFI's Holocaust Course*.

- Becoming a CUFI Congressional Liaison, where you can meet with your elected officials at local town halls and other events on key issues impacting the U.S.-Israel relationship.

- Joining our CUFI High School initiative or our CUFI on Campus chapters nationwide.

- Getting to know the Jewish community in your area. Building strong relationships matters, and we are stronger when we can work together on issues of common concern related to Israel.

CUFI is working across America and in our nation's capital to ensure that antisemitism is countered wherever it rears its ugly head. We accomplish this monumental task by:

- Ensuring efforts meant to destroy Israel with economic warfare are soundly defeated.

- Making certain that Israel has all the tools necessary to defeat any foes who threaten her.

- Countering antisemitism by working to ensure that the International Holocaust Remembrance Alliance (IHRA) definition of antisemitism is widely adopted. To date, 45 countries, 37 US state governments, and 96 city and county governments have adopted the definition and its contemporary examples.

Petitioning our government leaders to stand with Israel with executive orders and legislative action, such as:

1. After the urging of CUFI and allied groups, President Trump signed an Executive Order in December 2019, and he doubled down on the definition once reelected in 2025 by adopting the IHRA definition for use by the Department of Education.

2. CUFI continues to advocate for the Antisemitism Awareness Act. This legislation formally places the International Holocaust Remembrance Alliance's definition of antisemitism into law for guidance purposes when authorities are examining whether an underlying unlawful act was motivated by antisemitism.

The Antisemitism Awareness Act will assist authorities in contending with the mobs of people committing illegal and antisemitic acts while claiming they are not motivated by Jew hatred. This bill provides a clear definition, already acknowledged by most states nationwide. It allows authorities to use this guidance when investigating the underlying hate crime against Jews or pro-Israel advocates.

Why is this important? As an example, college students can still rant and rave against Israel and the Jewish people; these actions fall under our freedom of speech. But if they commit acts of harassment and vandalism while exercising this freedom, this legislation will empower authorities to determine when antisemitic acts have been committed, with disciplinary action to follow.

Contrary to some uninformed opinions, the Antisemitism Awareness Act does not outlaw the Bible; it does not even outlaw the cancer of antisemitism, but it will help expose Jew hatred in America. We know this to be true, and so should everyone in Congress, as it has effectively been in place since the 2019 Executive Order by President Trump.

The Jewish State is also being attacked not only militarily but economically in the boardrooms of major international companies thanks to the antisemitic and anti-Israel Boycott, Divestment, and Sanction (BDS) movement. There, too, CUFI has been at the forefront of shutting down these attacks.

> **Contrary to some uninformed opinions, the Antisemitism Awareness Act does not outlaw the Bible; it does not even outlaw the cancer of antisemitism, but it will help expose Jew hatred in America.**

At the time of this printing, 37 U.S. states have policies in place to ensure that if a company seeks to boycott Israel, it will not receive taxpayer dollars in those states.

Additionally, CUFI and Hagee Ministries have led a bipartisan initiative in Congress to ensure that the federal government aligns with these states. This establishes that any company participating in a boycott of Israel will no longer be eligible to receive federal contracts.

To this end, the Countering Hate Against Israel by Federal Contractors Act (CHAI) exists. We seek to advance this policy both legislatively and through the executive branch so that the BDS movement is once and for all shut down.

While CUFI and Hagee Ministries supports the yearly $3.8 billion in military assistance to Israel, the unprecedented October 7, 2023, attack and the ensuing multi-front war required a much bigger military response. As such, the United States, in conjunction with Israel, put forward a historic $14.3 billion emergency war supplement for Israel.

CUFI sprang into action, and in just seven days, we were able to mobilize 250 CUFI leaders from across the country to Washington on April 15–16 for an emergency fly-in to show support for this critical emergency military assistance package for Israel.

Our message was clear: love is not what you say but what you do.

House Speaker Johnson then told CUFI leaders, "We have to make certain that the entire world understands that Israel is not alone and that God is going to bless the nation that blesses Israel."

Shortly thereafter, on April 20, the House passed this package, followed by the Senate on April 23, and the president signed it into law on April 24, 2024. CUFI, Congress, and America sent an unequivocal message: Israel is not alone!

Across Europe, antisemitic threats and attacks skyrocketed after the October 7 Massacre. Reports surfaced of bomb threats to Jewish stores, firebombed synagogues, and demonstrations calling for Israel's eradication. Pogroms as far away as Australia have occurred.

America's institutions of higher learning suffered a 700% rise in the number of antisemitic incidents on their campuses between October and February relative to the same period a year earlier. The United Nations has continued to condemn Israel, and some of our own congressional leadership has denounced Israel's right to defend itself.

Israel is under attack by Jew hatred in all its many forms. This book's journey has come

> **CUFI, Congress, and America sent an unequivocal message: Israel is not alone!**

full circle. Remember God's vow to Amalek, which is a term used to describe any enemy of the Jewish people.

> *Then the L<small>ORD</small> said to Moses, "Write this for a memorial in the book and recount it in the hearing of Joshua, that I will utterly blot out the remembrance of Amalek from under heaven." And Moses built an altar and called its name, The-L<small>ORD</small>-Is-My-Banner; for he said, "Because the L<small>ORD</small> has sworn: the L<small>ORD</small> will have war with Amalek from generation to generation."*
> Exodus 17:14–16

As for me and my house — we will stand on God's side. Christians must unite as we comfort and defend Israel and the Jewish people. The time to support the Jewish nation is now! We must sound the alarm and declare, "NEVER AGAIN!"

From beginning to end, the Bible is a Zionist document mandating that all believers stand with and bless Israel and her people. God, the Creator of Heaven and earth, recorded the borders of Israel in sacred Scripture, and they will stand for eternity.

I pray that by the time you read this book, Operation Swords of Iron and Operation Iron Wall will have ended, Hamas and Hezbollah have been destroyed, Iran has been defused, all the surviving hostages have safely returned to their families, and the bodies of Israel's dead have been laid to rest in their eternal homeland.

The people of Israel are our family. Israel's sorrow is our sorrow, her pain is our pain, and her loss is our loss — family grieves together. Family also prays together, and the God of Abraham, Isaac, and Jacob has mandated Christians and Jews everywhere to pray for the peace of Jerusalem:

> *Pray for the peace of Jerusalem:*
> *"May they prosper who love you.*
> *Peace be within your walls,*
> *Prosperity within your palaces."*
> *For the sake of my brethren and companions,*
> *I will now say, "Peace be within you."*
> *Because of the house of the LORD our God*
> *I will seek your good.*
> Psalm 122:6–9

ENDNOTES

i. Jewish News Syndicate. "7,000 Gazans Took Part in Oct. 7 Attacks, New IDF Data Shows." *JNS.org*. Accessed April 17, 2025. https://www.jns.org/7000-gazans-took-part-in-oct-7-attacks-new-idf-data-shows/

ii. Goldenberg, Tia. "Hostages in Gaza Endure Another Winter as Their Families Plead for a Ceasefire." *Associated Press*, January 7, 2025. Updated 11:05 PM CST.

iii. Foundation for Defense of Democracies. "19,000 Rockets Launched at Israel Since Hamas's October 7 Atrocities." *FDD.org*, June 11, 2024. https://www.fdd.org/analysis/2024/06/11/19000-rockets-launched-at-israel-since-hamass-october-7-atrocities/

iv. Jewish News Syndicate. "90 Major Attacks Thwarted as Iran Fuels Unrest in Judea and Samaria." *JNS.org*, February 6, 2025.

v. "'Day of Rage': Tens of Thousands Protest across Mideast after Hamas Call. Demonstrators Rally in Multiple Cities, Burning Flags and Chanting for Israel's Destruction." *Times of Israel*. Accessed April 17, 2025.

vi. Srinath, Nell. "One Year Later, Campuses Ban Pro-Palestine Protests 'In All but Name.'" https://www.thefreelibrary.com/One+Year+Later%2c+Campuses+Ban+Pro-Palestine+Protests+%27In+All+But...-a0823389876 December 19, 2024, 11:21 AM.

vii. "Columbia federal contracts and grants worth billions at risk over campus antisemitism." *The Jerusalem Post*. Accessed April 17, 2025. https://www.jpost.com/diaspora/antisemitism/article-844605

viii. Runes, Dagobert D. *The War Against the Jew*. New York: Philosophical Library, 1942.

ix. Louis D. Brandeis Center. "31 Countries Adopt New Definition of Antisemitism That Includes Anti-Zionism." *The Tower*, June 3, 2016.

x. Lockshin, Rabbi Martin. "Haman's Antisemitism: What Did He Not Like About the Jews?" *TheTorah.com*, 2016. https://www.thetorah.com/article/hamans-antisemitism-what-did-he-not-like-about-the-jews.

xi. Brainly. "After Alexander the Great's Death, His Empire Was Divided into How Many Kingdoms?"

xii. "Antiochus Epiphanes—The Bible's Most Notoriously Forgotten Villain." *Bible History Daily*.

xiii. Flannery, Edward H. *The Anguish of the Jews: Twenty-Three Centuries of Anti-Semitism*. New York: Paulist Press, 1985, p. 13.

xiv. Ibid., p. 8.

xv. Josephus, Flavius. *History of the Jewish War*. (75–79 CE).

xvi. Christian History Institute. "325: The First Council of Nicaea." *Christian History*.

xvii. Eusebius. *Life of Constantine*, Vol. III, Ch. XVIII. In *Catholic Encyclopedia*.

xviii. Eusebius. *Life of Constantine*, Vol. III, Ch. XVIII. In *The Seven Ecumenical Councils*.

xix. Denova, Rebecca. "Christian Antisemitism in the Middle Ages & During the Reformation." *World History Encyclopedia*, December 7, 2023.

xx. Rothman, Lilly. "'It's Not That the Story Was Buried.' What Americans in the 1930s Really Knew About What Was Happening in Germany." *Time Magazine*, updated July 10, 2018. https://time.com/5327279/ushmm-americans-and-the-holocaust/

xxi. Ignatius of Antioch. *Epistle to the Magnesians* (98–117 A.D.).

xxii. Justin Martyr. *Dialogue With Trypho* 11. In *Ante-Nicene Fathers*, Vol. 1, p. 200.

xxiii. Chrysostom, John. *Against the Jews*, Homily 1.

xxiv. Charlotte. *Jewish Christians, Judaizers, and Anti-Judaism*. Minneapolis, MN: Fortress Press, 2010, pp. 234–254.

xxv. John Chrysostom, *Against the Jews*, Homily 1

xxvi. St. Augustine. *Confessions*, 12.14 (c. 354–430 A.D.).

xxvii. *Codex Theodosianus*. In *The Oxford Dictionary of Byzantium*. New York & Oxford: Oxford University Press, 1991, p. 475.

xxviii. Luther, Martin. "On the Jews and Their Lies" (1543). *Jewish Virtual Library*.

xxix. Calvin, John. Quoted in *The Calvin Handbook*, ed. Heman J. Selderhuis, trans. Henry J. Baron.

xxx. "Jewish Massacre Denounced: East Side Mass Meeting Plans to Help

Victims of Russians in Kishinev." *New York Times*, April 28, 1903, p. 6.

xxxi. "Jewish Ghetto, Venice." *Sacred Destinations*. http://www.sacred-destinations.com/italy/venice-ghetto

xxxii. *The Holocaust Explained: The Ghettos.*

xxxiii. Ibid.

xxxiv. *United States Holocaust Memorial Museum: Operation Reinhardt.*

xxxv. United States Holocaust Memorial Museum. "Protocols of the Elders of Zion."

xxxvi. Columbia School of International and Public Affairs. "Dr. Deborah Lipstadt Discusses How Antisemitism Threatens Democracy."

xxxvii. ADL. *Antisemitism Uncovered.*

xxxviii. Ibid.

xxxix. World Jewish Congress. "The Myth That Jews Spread Disease."

xl. Foa, Anna. *The Jews of Europe After the Black Death.* 2000, p. 146.

xli. World Jewish Congress. "The Myth That Jews Spread Disease."

xlii. AJC. *Global Trends in Conspiracy Theories Linking Jews with Coronavirus.*

xliii. Columbia School of International and Public Affairs. "Ambassador Deborah Lipstadt Discusses How Antisemitism Threatens Democracy."

xliv. Matthew Henry. *Commentary on John 10:10.*

xlv. *Enduring Word Commentary: John 10 - The Good Shepherd.*

xlvi. Britannica. "Mein Kampf, A Work by Hitler."

xlvii. BBC. *BBC History.*

xlviii. "Anti-Jewish Legislation in Prewar Germany." *Holocaust Encyclopedia.*

xlix. Noakes, Jeremy, and Geoffrey Pridham. *Documents on Nazism, 1919–1945.* New York: Viking Press, 1974, pp. 463–467.

l. "Examples of Antisemitic Legislation, 1933–1939." *United States Holocaust Memorial Museum.*

li. *The Night of Broken Glass.* United States Holocaust Memorial Museum, Washington, DC.

lii. "Quote from Hitler's Reichstag Speech."

liii. David B. Green, "This Day in Jewish History 1939: Hitler Makes First Call for Jews' 'Annihilation.'"

liv. "World Responses to Kristallnacht," from the story of the *St. Louis* and the controversy over the children's immigration bill sponsored by Senator Robert Wagner and Representative Edith Nourse Rogers.

lv. "U.S. Policy During the Holocaust: The Tragedy of S.S. *St. Louis* (May 13–June 20, 1939)." *Jewish Virtual Library*.

lvi. Robert Rosen, "Saving the Jews" (speech, Carter Center, Atlanta, Georgia, July 17, 2006).

lvii. "No One Wants the Jews: Remembering the St. Louis." *Aish*.

lviii. "World War II: Facts, Information, and Articles about World War II, 1939–1945."

lix. "Why Did the League of Nations Fail to Keep the Peace in the 1930s?" *Marked by Teachers*, International History.

lx. "Timeline of Events." United States Holocaust Memorial Museum.

lxi. Ibid.

lxii. "The Camps." *The Teachers Guide to the Holocaust*.

lxiii. *The Destruction of the European Jews*, 9.

lxiv. "The German Churches and the Nazi State." *Holocaust Encyclopedia*.

lxv. Elie Wiesel, interview with U.S. media, 1986.

lxvi. John F. Walvoord, *The Millennial Kingdom* (Grand Rapids: Dunham, 1959), 139.

lxvii. Theodor Herzl, *Der Judenstaat* (1896), 5.

lxviii. Ibid.

lxix. "Pre-State Israel: Arab Riots of the 1920s." *Jewish Virtual Library*.

lxx. Ibid.

lxxi. Ibid.

lxxii. Ibid., 56.

lxxiii. Ibid.

lxxiv. "JIMENA: Jews Indigenous to the Middle East and North Africa."

lxxv. *The Meir Amit Intelligence and Terrorism Information Center.*

lxxvi. David Patterson, *The Muslim Brotherhood and the Evolution of Jihadist Antisemitism*, Institute for the Study of Global Antisemitism and Policy.

lxxvii. Ibid.

lxxviii. "The Muslim Brotherhood White Paper." *The Investigative Project on Terrorism.*

lxxix. Ibid.

lxxx. *Jerusalem Center for Security and Foreign Affairs (JCFA)*, "Egypt Fears the Strengthening of the 'Muslim Brotherhood' Movement."

lxxxi. "Palestine Liberation Organization: The Original Palestine National Charter (1964)." *Jewish Virtual Library.*

lxxxii. Ibid.

lxxxiii. "Munich Olympic Massacre: Background & Overview (September 1972)." *Jewish Virtual Library.*

lxxxiv. "Israel's Wars & Operations: The Entebbe Rescue Operation (July 1976)." *Jewish Virtual Library.*

lxxxv. "First Lebanon War: Background & Overview (1982–1985)." *Jewish Virtual Library.*

lxxxvi. Ibid.

lxxxvii. Seth J. Frantzman, *Jerusalem Post*, November 2024.

lxxxviii. Israel Ministry of Foreign Affairs, "Wave of Terror 2015–2018."

lxxxix. "Palestinians Increase Payments to Terrorists to $403 Million." *Jerusalem Post*, March 2018.

xc. MEMRI, "Palestinian Authority President Mahmoud Abbas at Fatah Revolutionary Council Session: We Will Not Stop the Payments to the Prisoners and the Martyrs' Families," February 28, 2025.

xci. David Daoud, *On the Roots and Branches of Shi'a Antisemitism.*

xcii. Ibid.

xciii. "Hezbollah." *Counter Extremism Project.*

xciv. Ibid.

xcv. Ibid.

xcvi. "Iran Launches Festival to Celebrate Israel's 'Imminent Collapse.'" *Israel National News*, 2018.

xcvii. *The Institute for the Study of War*, "Israel's Victory in Lebanon."

xcviii. David Patterson, *The Muslim Brotherhood and the Evolution of Jihadist Antisemitism*, Institute for the Study of Global Antisemitism and Policy.

xcix. Abdullah Haidar Shai', "Hamas—Shattering of the Image." *Global Islamic Media Front and Dar al-Murabiteen Publications*, December 22, 2009.

c. Aaron Y. Zelin, "The Gaza War Has Jump-Started a Weakened al-Qaeda." *The Washington Institute for Near East Policy*.

ci. "ISIS." *Counter Extremism Project*.

cii. "Hamas: Background & Overview." *Jewish Virtual Library*.

ciii. *Israel for Critical Thinkers*, 87–91.

civ. Ibid., 96.

cv. "Hamas War Tactics: Attacks from Civilian Centers (2016)," unclassified by the Israel Defense Forces. *Jewish Virtual Library*.

cvi. "Fatah Vows Not to Let Hamas 'Replicate Its Actions' in West Bank, Slams Iran." *Times of Israel*, January 12, 2025.

cvii. "Israel Missed Obvious Signs Hamas Was About to Attack." *The Wall Street Journal*, February 27, 2025.

cviii. Kelsey Davenport, "The Coming Iranian Nuclear Challenge in 2025." *The Iran Primer*, United States Institute of Peace, January 13, 2025.

cix. "Military Assistance to Israel." Marco Rubio, Secretary of State, March 1, 2025.

cx. *Foundation for the Defense of Democracies*, "U.S. Grants Iran Sanctions Waiver Worth $10 Billion," March 14, 2024.

cxi. *2017 Audit of Antisemitic Incidents*. Anti-Defamation League, February 27, 2018.

cxii. Anti-Defamation League, https://www.adl.org/audit-antisemitic-incidents.

cxiii. Zev Stub, "Survey: 83% of Jewish US College Students Have Experienced Antisemitism Since Oct. 7." *Times of Israel*, February 2, 2025.

cxiv. "Pandemic of Antisemitism Taking Shape Worldwide, Even Threatens America, Warns Top US Jewish Leader." *Times of Israel*, February 2017.

cxv. Yehuda Bauer.

NOTES

LEARN MORE

CHRISTIANS UNITED FOR ISRAEL

Christians United for Israel is the foremost Christian organization educating and empowering millions of Americans to speak and act with one voice in defense of Israel and the Jewish people. CUFI's diversity across political, ethnic, generational, and denominational lines maximizes our impact in communities, media, on campus, and in our nation's capital. CUFI is committed to confronting indifference and combating antisemitism in all its forms wherever it may be found. For more information, visit CUFI.org.

HAGEE MINISTRIES

Hagee Ministries exists to take all the Gospel to all the world and to every generation, boldly proclaiming Biblical truth and demonstrating the love of Christ through action. With unwavering support for Israel and a deep commitment to God's covenant, the ministry blesses the Jewish people in alignment with Scripture. Through global media outreach, discipleship resources, and compassionate initiatives like the Sanctuary of Hope, Hagee Ministries ministers to both the spiritual and practical needs of individuals, fulfilling its mission to serve, equip, and stand in obedience to God's Word. For more information, visit jhm.org.

ABOUT JOHN HAGEE

John Hagee is the founder and senior pastor of Cornerstone Church in San Antonio, Texas, a nondenominational evangelical church with more than 22,000 active members. Pastor Hagee has served the Lord in the Gospel ministry for 67 years. He is the author of more than 45 books, including several *New York Times* bestsellers, his latest being *To Save America: The Ten Commandments*. Pastor Hagee is the founder and chairman of Christians United for Israel (CUFI), with over 10 million members. Hagee Ministries reaches millions worldwide through its television program, provides refuge and care to mothers and babies through the Sanctuary of Hope, and steadfastly supports Israel and the Jewish people in alignment with God's mandate to believers.

Engage with Pastor John Hagee Online:

Hagee Ministries
jhm.org

CUFI
cufi.org

Facebook
HageeMinistries

X
PastorJohnHagee
HageeMinistries

Instagram
PastorJohnHagee
HageeMinistries

Amazon Author Page
Find other books by Pastor John Hagee and engage further by leaving a review to encourage other readers.